— ❧ THE ❧ —
PLANT-BASED
DOG FOOD
REVOLUTION

THE
PLANT-BASED
DOG FOOD
REVOLUTION

WITH 50 RECIPES

MIMI KIRK & LISA KIRK

DOG PHOTOGRAPHY BY HANNAH KIRK
FOOD PHOTOGRAPHY BY MIKE MENDELL

THE COUNTRYMAN PRESS

A division of W. W. Norton & Company

Independent Publishers Since 1923

The information in this book is not in place of seeing your veterinarian or diagnosing any disease or condition your dog might have. Before starting your pet on any changes to their diet or giving them supplements, please check with your veterinarian. The recipes in this book are to benefit a dog's diet along with your regular veterinarian care. Every effort has been made to ensure that the information and the recipes in this book are nutritionally sound and balanced. The authors and publisher are not liable for any adverse effects your dog may experience while eating plant-based foods and/or our recipes.

For information about permission to reproduce selections from this book, write to Permissions, The Countryman Press, 500 Fifth Avenue, New York, NY 10110

For information about special discounts for bulk purchases, please contact W. W. Norton Special Sales at specialsales@wwnorton.com or 800-233-4830

Manufacturing by Versa Press
Book design by Endpaper Studio
Production manager: Devon Zahn

Library of Congress Cataloging-in-Publication Data
Names: Kirk, Mimi, 1938– author. | Kirk, Lisa (Canine herbalist), author.
Title: The plant-based dog food revolution : with 50 recipes / Mimi Kirk, Lisa Kirk.
Description: New York, NY : The Countryman Press, a division of
W. W. Norton & Company, {2019} | Includes index.
Identifiers: LCCN 2018042504 | ISBN 9781682682715 (paperback)
Subjects: LCSH: Dogs—Food—Recipes. | Dogs--Nutrition.
Classification: LCC SF427.4 .K535 2019 | DDC 636.7/083—dc23
LC record available at https://lccn.loc.gov/2018042504

The Countryman Press
www.countrymanpress.com

A division of W. W. Norton & Company, Inc.
500 Fifth Avenue, New York, NY 10110
www.wwnorton.com

978-1-68268-271-5 (pbk.)

10 9 8 7 6 5 4 3 2 1

Some people talk to animals. Not many listen though. That's the problem.

—A. A. MILNE, *WINNIE-THE-POOH*

———o———

To Bianca, best friend, foodie, sous-chef, and taste tester.

Contents

—— o ——

Foreword by Armaiti May, DVM and CVA

———o———

IN AN AGE WHERE RECALLS OF PET FOOD HAVE BECOME ALL TOO COMMON AND dog guardians are increasingly conscientious about what their four-legged friends are consuming, this timely book serves as a practical guide for promoting true wellness in our canine companions, thus warding off diseases such as cancer, which are affecting an alarmingly high percentage of dogs nowadays. As a practicing veterinarian for thirteen years, I have seen many dogs suffering from allergies, including to chicken and beef, which are greatly alleviated by switching to a plant-based diet. I have also seen far too many dogs afflicted with cancer who were euthanized because of it. The oath to protect animals from suffering that I took upon graduating veterinary school resonates deeply with me and I feel it is my duty to prevent suffering, not only for companion animals but farmed animals as well. Choosing a vegan diet for myself to prevent the suffering of farmed animals, along with the environmental and health benefits, made sense.

For some time during the earlier part of my academic career, I felt an internal conflict feeding meat to omnivorous dogs, since I did not want to cause the death of one animal to feed another. However, when I looked into the issue more thoroughly and became familiar with the science behind nutrition, I was amazed to learn about some significant health concerns around feeding dogs a conventional meat-based diet and I came to realize that well-balanced, plant-based diets not only satisfy dogs' nutritional requirements but also provide a much cleaner diet in terms of exposure to toxins. These toxins include carcinogenic chemicals and heavy metals such as arsenic, dioxins, DDT, PCBS, and mercury, to name a few, which concentrate in animal tissue and bioaccumulate up the food chain.

It's certainly understandable that the popular view amongst many dog guardians and veterinarians is that dogs require meat in their diet. However, the reality is that dogs are omnivores and they may not need meat in their diets. In fact, there are numerous commercially available, AAFCO-approved, plant-based diets that can meet the dietary requirements of shelter dogs, while *improving* the health of the dogs, while also addressing some of the most urgent issues of our time. We are sleepwalking off a cliff with regards to climate change, the availability of fresh drinking water, and a build-up of dangerous, carcinogenic toxins in our bodies, the bodies of our animal companions, and the environment. A United Nations study entitled "Livestock's Long Shadow" points to animal agriculture as the leading cause of climate change. Today both humans *and* dogs face life-threatening environmental problems and—given that scientific evidence supports the viability and benefits of nutritionally complete and balanced plant-based diets for dogs—it is important to find viable options for nourishing our canine companions without causing unnecessary harm to other creatures or the planet that we all call home. This book provides a wealth of vitally important information for dog guardians and features delicious, nourishing, homemade plant-based recipes which are certain to delight the palate—of both dogs and their human caretakers alike.

Introduction

———o———

AT THE SIMPLE WAG OF A TAIL, THE BOND BETWEEN YOU AND YOUR PUP IS IMME-diate and lasting. It acts as a silent agreement that they will be your café companion, morning stroll sidekick, and if lucky, bedmate. It's a built-in friendship destined to last.

According to the American Pet Products Association, there are more than 80 mil-lion household dogs in the United States, and in 2016 Americans spent more than $60 billion on their pets, buying luxury beds, blingy dog collars, dog carriers, toys, clothes, and pet bowls, proving there is no end to how much people love their pets.

Furthering man's unyielding love for his pooch, a *New York Times* article, "When the Dog Decides Where You Live," revealed that some pet parents will spend hun-dreds of thousands of dollars to live close to their dog walkers, sacrificing location to find the right apartment for their dog's happiness. This may sound strange to a non-dog lover but to those who consider dogs to be part of the family, caring for your dog's comfort and health is perfectly normal. Parents want to keep their dogs healthy and happy from puppy to senior years.

We love our dogs so much that we walk them daily, give them a nice comfy bed (or let them sleep in ours), put their sweaters or jackets on when the weather turns cold, give them shelter, and scratch their bellies. Despite all this love and care, the National Cancer Institute's Comparative Oncology Program reports that more than half of US dogs get cancer and other diseases. They may become overweight, be prescribed medi-cations, and seem to need constant medical care. Indeed, canine pharmaceutical companies are becoming as large as human pharmaceutical companies. Nonetheless, dogs continue to get sick and it's painful to watch. Something is just not right!

Most commercial dog food brands will tell you that they are fortified with vitamins and antioxidants to keep your dog living healthier and longer. These foods, however, are full of chemically processed mystery ingredients. The Joint Expert Committee on Food Additives (a cooperation between the World Health Organization and the Food and Agriculture Organization of the United Nations) worries that exposure to acrylamide and other compounds that have been found in commercial dog food may cause cancer. We know dogs are not picky eaters. They will eat out of garbage cans when left to their own devices. But, as our dogs' guardian, it's our responsibility to choose what's best for our domesticated companions when it comes to their food. Fresh, organic homemade meals are a great improvement from that chemically processed mystery dog chow. And while there is more research being done on the ingredients that go into commercial dog food, we feel it is always better to be safe than sorry and feed your dogs organic homemade food.

Some may choose to feed their dog a plant-based diet for ethical and/or health reasons, and some believe their dog needs meat. For those not ready to transition their dogs to an all plant-based diet, our recipes will power up any prepared foods your dog currently eats, providing extensive nutrients to keep them healthy.

The following information includes all of our findings, research, and interviews with experts on how best to feed your dog a plant-based diet. We leave the final decision up to you to find your own comfort zone.

We have embarked upon a controversial subject: a plant-based diet for dogs. With an open mind and a love for your dog, we hope you will be excited to learn what we discovered when we sorted through reams of technical data, compared notes with notable pet nutritionists, and shared many conversations with vegan dog parents and experts in the field including scientists, researchers, dog food formulators, and veterinarians.

What are the right foods to feed your dog? Giant pet food companies spend millions of dollars on advertising to list the dangers of feeding our pets homemade human food—regardless of all the information we've uncovered stating dogs can do very well with homemade plant food and proper supplementation. Could this information be spread to protect dog food companies' bottom line?

In part, it's true: Not all food fit for humans is good for your dog, but don't disregard the health benefits of properly homemade, plant-based dog food.

We hope this book will enlighten you on what is good human food for your dog versus what is not, and provide you with some delicious plant-based recipes that you might just want to share with your dog.

We've tested our recipes on dogs, eaten the food ourselves, served it to company, researched every ingredient, and crosschecked them to bring your furry friend the most up-to-date, balanced, organic, fresh plant based meals for the twenty-first century. Since all dogs are different, even in the same family, some dogs will need additional supplementation (see Chapter Two on *Supplementation*, page 42).

We all love our canine companions and want to feed them only the very best food just as we want to eat nutritionally wholesome food ourselves. When we discovered what went into many top-selling, name-brand dog foods, and how many dogs get cancer, tumors, heart issues, bone disease, and many other illnesses—and are on daily prescription medication—we had to speak up and help revolutionize the way dog food is viewed and consumed.

HOW THINGS HAVE CHANGED

Dogs have been leading the good life. They are not out hunting prey—they are sitting at their bowl waiting for you to feed them. They don't get exercise like wolves in the wild because they have you to take care of all their needs and walk them on their leash every day. One could say it was natural for humans to hunt and eat meat at one time in history, but we are in the twenty-first century and new research has allowed us to know more about our eating habits and how to make healthier choices. For decades, we've been told we need to eat meat to get our protein, but more recent research, published on *Medical News Today*, suggests that both humans and dogs can get protein from other sources including dark leafy greens, nuts and seeds, legumes, quinoa, and spirulina. Look at endurance athletes living on a plant-based diet: Serena Williams, Tim Shieff, Scott Jurek, David Carter, Patrik Baboumian, and Griff Whalen, just to name a few. They display their muscle, win contests, and are completely healthy—and yes, they get enough protein. Throughout this book, you will learn about vegan dogs living and thriving as well.

Human health depends on the quality of food we consume, and the same goes for our dogs. It has been shown that when we eat an organic, plant-based diet and stop eating processed foods, which are full of chemicals, health often improves. We hope

to broaden your thinking regarding plant-based meals for your dog and maybe even improve your own diet as well.

To those who are looking for a compassionate alternative to feeding their dog a meat-based diet, we thank you for opening up your hearts and minds as you consider a different way to support your dog's good health without harming other species and the environment.

THE INSPIRATION FOR THIS BOOK

Many vegans who choose to eat a cruelty-free and compassionate diet face an ethical dilemma when feeding animal byproducts to their dogs. With so much conflicting information on how best to feed one's dog, vegans have been faced with their conscience. They have been told not to impose their lifestyle choice on their dog, as dogs need meat to be healthy.

We've heard people say, "Get a rabbit" if you don't want to feed your dog meat. Getting rabbits in cages instead of rescuing dogs from shelters is not the answer. Vegans love all animals and without them, many dogs and cats would be euthanized in shelters or just left on the streets.

It would be great if we could just feed our dog exactly what we eat, but table scraps will not be enough for their nutritional needs and some foods are toxic to dogs. To develop the recipes in this book, we worked with food formulators and vegan veterinarians so you will be sure your pup's nutritional needs are met. Many dogs enjoy improved health when they are switched to a plant-based diet. Dogs who eat commercial or standard animal-based diets can also improve their health when more plant foods are included into their daily meals. It takes careful attention to feed your dog a homemade, plant-based diet, and in this book, we provide you with the best up-to-date information so you can feel confident that your dog is getting the proper nutrients. Plus, with a plant-based diet, your pup will leave a smaller pawprint on the planet.

WHAT YOU CAN EXPECT FROM *THE PLANT-BASED DOG FOOD REVOLUTION*

When we started on our journey to find out if plant-based foods were good for dogs, we also wanted to know if plants were necessary in their diet. In 2005, a study conducted at Purdue University showed that adding fresh vegetables to dry commercial kibble prevented or slowed down bladder cancer. They tested two groups of dogs. One group ate only dry kibble and the other had vegetables added to their kibble. The study concluded that dogs who ate green leafy vegetables or broccoli reduced the risk of developing bladder cancer by 90 percent and dogs that consumed any yellow or orange vegetables, such as carrots, reduced their risk by 70 percent. This study showed that dogs have evolved to digest plant matter and assimilate the nutrients they provide.

We also found that it's not just processed commercial food that affects our dogs' health, but the lack of fresh food and nutrients in their diet. Although each dog may have different needs, fresh food is important to maintain ultimate health. Like humans, dogs require real food, not just synthetically processed, high-carbohydrate foods. Although vegan dogs are a more recent subject, one study conducted by veterinarian Andrew Knight showed that it is possible for dogs to survive and thrive on a plant-based diet as long as they are getting the nutrients they need. Plant-based food and the proper supplements may even combat diseases including cancer, infections, diabetes, arthritis, and cataracts, to name a few.

We researched all sides of the controversy and found that some experts believe dogs are scavenger carnivores, meaning they eat what they find in the wild. However, other studies show that domesticated dogs can be—and are—actually omnivores, meaning their dietary needs can be met by consuming a nutritionally balanced plant-based diet and proper supplements. Their bodies can digest and obtain the nutrients from plant foods. One noteworthy example is a 25-year-old Border Collie named Bramble, whose diet consisted of rice, lentils, and organic vegetables. She earned her place in the *Guinness Book of World Records* as the world's oldest living dog. We interviewed Bramble's parent, Anne Heritage, and you can read her story on page 19.

Just as new information for human diets is brought to light daily, so is new information for dogs. *Small Animal Clinical Nutrition* (5th Edition), by Michael Hand, and the National Research Council for Nutrient Requirements for Dogs and Cats confirm that a properly balanced plant-based diet without any animal products will supply your dog with all the essential nutrients needed to be healthy. We emphasize the words *complete* and *balanced* because simply feeding plant food to your dog might not be enough for them to get all their minerals, amino acids, protein, and nutrients to keep them healthy. We have carefully formulated our recipes with expert help to make sure your dog companion gets the very best at each meal, and we recommend supplements as needed. Balancing food and supplements is the answer to a healthier dog.

The main goal of the book is to keep our pups healthy and happy while respecting the Earth and all living beings. We show you how simple it is to make homemade food for your dog, assuring you of what goes into each meal. If you are a busy person, just follow our easy plan for preparing meals for a week at a time (see page 45). We make it efficient for you to prepare homemade food, and your dog will benefit from each meal. We provide the latest information on how to increase your dog's health by enhancing their nutritional needs.

Not everyone will be convinced to switch their dog to a vegan diet, but the information in this book will help to improve your dog's current diet and health while dispelling some myths about adding fresh plant foods to their meals. For those already feeding their dog a plant-based diet, you will learn what is needed for a well-balanced meal. If you ever wondered if commercial dog food might not be the healthiest for your pup, then *The Plant-Based Dog Food Revolution* will shed light on the pitfalls of commercial dog food and what you can do to improve your dog's overall health and well-being.

Even if you only feed your dog our plant-based recipes three days a week, it could give them the added nutrients they may be lacking in their regular daily meals.

The Plant-Based Dog Food Revolution provides easy well-balanced and affordable recipes including basic bowl meals, treats, and smoothies, as well as customized tricks for quick nutrients featured in our homemade mixes, SuperBoost, SuperSeedDust, and SuperYeastDust, which can be sprinkled on any meal. No preservatives, colorings, additives, GMO, or soy is used in our meals. Recipes contain human-grade fresh organic vegetables, fruits, sea vegetables, lentils, oatmeal, beans, seeds, and herbs. We also include a list of medicinal herbs such as turmeric, known to decrease inflammation, increase balanced energy, and aid in digestion. Snacks and chews contain flaxseed meal and vegetables rich with nutrients.

There are many vegan dogs living healthy, happy lives. They are thriving without harming other animals for their food. Homemade dog food, when prepared the right way, can help your pup enjoy a strong, healthy life. Here are some stories of vegan dogs written by their parents.

── ೩ ANNE HERITAGE AND BRAMBLE ೭ ──

Bramble, a Welsh Collie, lived to the age of twenty-five years old and, at the time of her death, was the world's oldest dog. Bramble was a vegan and Anne Heritage was Bramble's caretaker. We had the honor of catching up with Anne and hearing her story. She currently spends time disseminating information about vegan dog food while also taking part in environmental campaigning in Somerset, England, where the landscape is under siege from construction. She also promotes her book, *Bramble; The Dog who wanted to live forever*.

I was born in Somerset, UK. Dogs in my care lived long lives. Bramble was from a rescue center. My other companions lived to nineteen and twenty years old and were vegan as well. I attribute their longevity to a care regime that includes organic vegan dog food, a lot of exercise, stress control, and recognizing the mental health implications for captive animals. I addressed this by treating them with respect and sufficient attention. I recognized that dogs are individuals with emotional lives and unique emotional landscapes and personalities. I also recognized that dogs are autonomous creatures—not pets or belongings.

When I rescued Bramble, she was eighteen months old. I was already vegan for animal rights reasons and so I wanted to feed dogs in my care cruelty-free. I also did not want to feed my dog food not fit for human consumption.

In order to feed your dog a vegan diet, you should read up about what vitamins, minerals, and other elements dogs need in their diets. Humans and dogs can share many foods, but be aware that not all human foods can be eaten by dogs—some can be poisonous for them. For example, chocolate, onions, grapes, and avocados can be eaten by us but could kill dogs. If you aren't sure, don't feed it to them. I believe garlic is poisonous to dogs. People argue about it, but is it worth risking?

Feed them organic foods exclusively—or whenever possible. Pesticides can build up in dog bodies and cause illnesses, including cancer. Homemade is best, as you can control what they are eating and build health instead of disease.

In forty years, I never fed any processed oils to dogs in my care. Oil is better fed via seeds like flax or chia. Too many cooked processed oils can cause pancreatitis.

I would urge people to home cook organic, carefully sourced, or home-grown produce. If you grow your own food, your health will benefit as well. To ensure there is enough calcium in a dog's diet, you can feed foods including dandelion leaves, collard greens, broccoli, mustard greens, and beet greens. Kidney beans are also high in calcium.

I always use yeast extract in dog food. I found yeast flakes may cause upset stomachs in some dogs, so I cook organic brown rice with one teaspoon of yeast extract in the water, which gets absorbed into the rice and provides B vitamins, including B12.

One version of Bramble's dinner:

1 mug organic whole-grain brown rice

½ mug organic red split lentils

½ mug vegan beef flavor textured vegetable protein

½ teaspoon yeast extract

1 mug organic vegetables, such as carrots, cabbage, and broccoli

1 teaspoon organic fresh or dried mint

½ teaspoon turmeric

1 teaspoon pre-soaked chia seeds, or ½ teaspoon flaxseed powder

DIRECTIONS

Put all ingredients except chia seeds or flaxseed powder in a large pan and cover with filtered water. Bring to a boil. Simmer on low heat for approximately one hour. Give it a stir on and off. Once all foods are cooked, drain and cool. Then add pre-soaked chia seeds or flaxseed powder and give it a good stir. This will feed two dogs one large meal. You can eat it too!

I cared for seven dogs for over forty years. Bramble liked to pick blackberries off of bushes in season. Dreadlock ate two ripe bananas each day. (He would thoughtfully shake them by skin first in case they were still alive!) Sally was partial to berries. Floyd enjoyed apples, pits removed first because they contain cyanide which can kill dogs. I think raw fruits and vegetables that are edible for dogs are helpful for them because of the enzymes in raw food.

Assisting dogs isn't just about proper feeding. Once you are feeding them healthy vegan food, get them outside where they can enjoy running about and exercising. You are their caretaker and should respect them. They are intelligent, loyal, loving, and kind. Enjoy their company as they enjoy yours.

CHAPTER ONE

About Plant-Based Dog Food

———o———

"Let food be thy medicine and medicine be thy food."

—HIPPOCRATES

IT'S BEEN PROVEN THAT WHEN HUMANS CHANGE THEIR DIETS TO A PLANT-based fresh food lifestyle, they get healthier and can even rid themselves of major health problems. "Vegetarian" and "vegan" are not fringe or foreign words anymore. Eating quality organic foods and eliminating processed foods from our diet both play a large role in helping us achieve—and maintain—good health. Negative information and recalls of packaged food for dogs have prompted many conscious eaters to be more concerned about healthy ways to feed their dogs as well.

Just as people often improve their health by changing to a plant-based diet, so can dogs. We know dogs that have been cured of allergies, stomach disorders, skin disease, and a multitude of illnesses, and a plant-based diet is a great catalyst for health. Dogs that eat plant-based foods, including proper supplements, can obtain all the amino acids and nourishment they need to stay in tip-top physical shape.

Some dogs eat dry kibble, canned food, and maybe a table treat here and there for their entire life, but how do you think your health would look like if you ate the same food daily? Variety in our dog's diet is very important because different nutrients and vitamins come from different foods. It's not just what they eat in one meal, but most important, what they eat on a weekly basis. Making home-cooked meals for our furry loved one or adding fresh foods to their existing meals will give us peace of mind that our dog's health is in good hands. With a proper diet, our dog will benefit from an improved immune system, healthy skin and coat, and enjoy a long active life. We would like to see your dog enjoy their senior years and have youthful vitality.

There are a number of packaged vegan dog foods sold today, and some are good. We are happy to see commercial vegan dog foods now available, but there are also some tested brands that do not meet the AAFCO (Association of American Feed Control Officials) standards, meaning they do not meet all the necessary nutritional needs. Some brands, for example, may contain soybeans, which could be GMO and cause allergies. Please avoid soy products that are not organic. Even if you use some soy, use it sparingly, and stay away from artificial preservatives. Read labels, ask questions, and do your research. All packaged foods have been processed and may not be the healthiest choice for your best friend. If you purchase commercial vegan dog food, please consider adding our fresh recipes and Dusts and Boosts (see page 143) to be sure your dog is getting fresh live vegetables and fruits for complete nutritional and digestive needs.

Here is why homemade meals are best. You get to purchase organic quality food; it's freshly made; you may add the proper amount of SuperBoost, SuperDusts, and any supplements appropriate for your dog; and most of all, you can prepare their meal with love. What dog wouldn't be devoted to that?

BEST FRIENDS DESERVE BETTER

The commercial dog food problem caught the attention of Dr. Oz, who featured the story "What's Really in Your Pet Food and Does It Matter?," exposing how unhealthy the ingredients in commercial dog food and dog treats are.

In the beginning, dogs ate scraps from our table. Then came along the commercial pet food industry wanting to convince us that their dog food was better and more balanced. In the 1960s, the lobbying group The Pet Food Institute started a campaign claiming that commercially processed kibble was the best and only food to feed our dogs. The campaign was hugely successful, and even though dogs today are not living

longer or without diseases, pet owners continue to buy commercial food—and veterinarians continue to promote it.

Veterinarians are taught how to treat disease and perform surgeries; they are trained in pharmacology, anatomy, emergency care, and all aspects of veterinary medicine. But we kept hearing from the ones we talked to that something was missing: They had very little training in nutrition. And the little training they did have came from dog food company representatives. Dog food manufacturers, who often sell dog food directly to veterinary clinics, tell veterinarians that home-cooked diets are unbalanced and potentially harmful and to caution their clients to avoid them, in favor of products they are selling.

In the past several years, recalls of commercial dog food have caused distrust and alarm. Some of the recalls are from trusted major companies who told us their products were the best to feed our dogs. In 2018, one dog food brand recalled several of its products because euthanizing drugs were found in the meat portion of the dog food. If you've ever wondered why some packaged dog foods and treats are marked "Not for Human Consumption," it's because US Department of Agriculture Inspectors have found that many supermarket dog foods contain animal parts that may be from dead, dying, diseased, or disabled animals. Who wants to eat that? No one should have to eat that!

Hidden additives uncovered

Even when you read labels, not all ingredients are listed on the package, including fats and sugars. Furthermore, some dog foods have been found to contain restaurant grease with dangerous free radicals, trans fatty acids, heavy metals, bacterial protozoa, hormones, preservatives, GMO, and antibiotic residues. Even when we do our best to buy healthy dog food, it may still be tainted with animal byproducts and derivatives, hormones, pesticides, antibiotics, additives, artificial colorants, sugars, unknown fillers, and propylene glycol—a clear viscous liquid used as a moistening agent and solvent in pharmaceutical preparations. This is enough to make any dog lover have serious concerns about what they're feeding their furry friend.

How do commercial foods harm our dogs?

According to some research, nearly half of all dogs will develop cancer. Dogs also suffer from IBS, arthritis, acid reflux, diabetes, heart disease, anemia, bone inflammation, seizures, epilepsy, and hundreds of other diseases. Our dogs need vitamins, nutrients, and enzymes just like we do, but with processed dog food, much of these essentials are long gone. The lack of nutrients, paired with the presence of chemicals and other additives, is playing havoc on our dogs' health.

HOW CAN WE HELP OUR DOGS GET AND STAY HEALTHY?

We interviewed some of the most important researchers and veterinarians to help us formulate our recipes. Although each dog is different when it comes to their health, here is what some of the holistic veterinarians and experts have to say.

Rodney Habib

No one loves dogs more than Rodney Habib. Rodney Habib is a blogger, lecturer, and the founder of the world's largest pet health page on Facebook, *Planet Paws*. He's the creator of a documentary series on the canine cancer epidemic ravaging the planet, *The Dog Cancer Series*. He has also filmed the documentary *The Truth About Pet Cancer*, with Ty Bollinger of *The Truth About Cancer* series. Rodney recently established the Paws For Change Foundation to raise money through charitable donations in order to further education and research in the areas of animal nutrition and the role of nutraceuticals, herbs, and natural healing in promoting animal longevity and wellbeing.

Rodney is a passionate researcher. You can catch his TEDx Talk, "Why Don't Dogs Live Forever," online and check out his Planet Paws, Paws for Change, and The Dog Cancer Series websites to learn more about his work.

We really appreciate Rodney giving us this interview because he is not a vegan. Rodney said that if you are going to write a plant-based dog food book, you have to make it the best because vegans need to know how to balance meals if they are feeding their dog no animal products. He does agree that fresh food is best and vegetables are important in a dog's diet.

Mimi and Lisa: *You travel the world advocating for dog welfare. How did your passion for dog health begin?*

Rodney Habib: It took two tragic circumstances in my life to get me on the path of helping dogs and cats. I got my first cat in 2007. My cat was affected by the Melamine recall. This contamination was in pet food imported from China. Thousands of pets were dying. My cat's kidneys were shot. Then in 2008 I got my first dog, Sandy. I ran to the market to get her some food and saw chicken jerky for dogs. They had all different kinds—some for brain-power, some for joints, and another for longevity. I bought all these jerkies and ended up destroying my dog's kidneys within 45 days. It really did something to me and I refused to allow Sandy's life to be in vain and that's when I started advocating for dogs. This is really what put me on the path and this is the reason I work so hard to inspire the world and to help other dogs.

M&L: *What is the main ingredient you believe can keep dogs living long and healthy?*
RH: I'd love to think there was just one thing. I love turmeric, but I came to realize very quickly while on this dog cancer awareness journey that it's not just one thing that keeps dogs healthy. Where I am today with this, sitting with top researchers and scientists as well as people with the longest living dogs, is that it's not a one-food ingredient that keeps our dogs healthy, but a one-life ingredient. What all these longest-living dogs have in common is calorie restriction. It was the common thread with all these dogs. The longest-living dogs eat one meal a day and get massive amounts of exercise. Bramble, who was a vegan/vegetarian dog, exercised 2 hours a day. Bramble lived to be twenty-five. Brian McClaren's dog, an Australian Kelpie named Maggie, lived to be thirty and she ran all day, following Brian around the farm while he drove his tractor. Maggie ran about 12½ miles a day. What this exercise did was it helped burn sugar and insulin. Besides calorie restriction and exercise, every interview and conversation I've done with the longest-living dog parents said they fed their dog some fresh food at each meal.

M&L: *What are your thoughts about dogs eating the same food day after day? Do you think they get enough nutrition in one formulated meal or do they need variety?*
RH: Variety in your dog's food is important, but there are many conflicting ideas. There is a model where some people say dogs need to eat as wolves do in the wild. Others believe adding fresh vegetables to our dogs' meals is important for their overall health regardless of whether they eat meat or dry kibble. I've interviewed over a dozen people with the longest-living dogs and I've read lots of data and the outcome is that all the longest-living dogs were fed fresh food.

M&L: *If people are feeding their dogs a vegan diet, how can they be sure their dog is getting enough nutrients?*

RH: The AVMA (American Veterinary Medical Association) tested commercially bagged and canned vegan food and concluded that most diets assessed in their study were not compliant with AAFCO (Association of American Feed Control Officials) labeling regulations, and there were concerns regarding adequacy of amino acids content. The problem is if you are going to feed your dog a vegan homemade diet, it better be fresh, whole, organic, bioavailable food.

You can have the USDA analyze a head of broccoli one year, but it does not mean that head of broccoli will have the same calcium content the next year. It can even be different depending on the soil it was grown in. If someone chooses to feed their dog a vegan homemade diet, it must be appropriately formulated and balanced and, when preparing the recipe, it must be followed to the letter. Switching one food for another could change the balance of the meal.

Andrew Knight, BSc (Vet Biol), BVMS, CertAW, MANZCVS, DipECAWBM (AWSEL), DipACAW, PhD, FRCVS, SFHEA

Andrew Knight is a very busy man. He is Professor of Animal Welfare and Ethics, and Director of the Centre for Animal Welfare, at the University of Winchester; a European and RCVS Veterinary Specialist in Animal Welfare Science, Ethics and Law; an American Veterinary Specialist in Animal Welfare; and a Senior Fellow of the UK Higher Education Academy.

Excluding abstracts and letters, Andrew has over 65 academic publications and a series of YouTube videos on animal issues. These include an extensive series examining the contributions to human healthcare of animal experiments, which formed the basis for his 2010 PhD and his 2011 book, *The Costs and Benefits of Animal Experiments*. Andrew's other publications have examined the contributions of the livestock sector to climate change, vegetarian companion animal diets, the animal welfare standards of veterinarians, and the latest evidence about animal cognitive and related abilities, and the resultant moral implications. His informational websites include www.animalexperiments.info, www.humanelearning.info, and www.vegepets.info.

Mimi and Lisa: *Let's get right at our main question. Can dogs thrive on a vegan diet?*
Andrew Knight: Dogs may be biologically classified as omnivores, due to their ability to subsist on a mixed diet of animal- and plant-based material in their wild natural environments. But, as domesticated omnivores, their nutritional needs are easier to meet on a vegan or vegetarian diet. There is absolutely no scientific reason why a balanced diet comprised entirely of plant, mineral, and synthetically based ingredients cannot meet all of the requirements dogs need to thrive.

Whatever combination of fresh plant, mineral, or synthetically based ingredients is used, diets should be formulated to meet the palatability, nutritional, and bioavailability requirements.

M&L: *Why do you think so many dogs get human diseases?*
AK: As a veterinarian, I believe that diseases such as cancer, kidney, liver, and heart failure are far more common than they should be, and that many of these diseases are likely to be exacerbated or directly caused by the numerous hazardous ingredients of commercial meat-based dog diets. Kidney disease, for example, is one of the top three killers of companion animals, and is aggravated by the extra load placed on the kidneys by the high-protein content and poor-quality ingredients of many meat-based diets. Left untreated, kidney disease may result in the systemic buildup of toxins, leading to loss of appetite, uremic poisoning, vomiting, neurological disorders, and death.

Our widespread reliance on meat-based diets causes enormous suffering, ill health, and premature deaths for literally billions of companion animals annually. With a wide range of healthy vegan alternatives, a dog can live a healthy, thriving life.

M&L: *Can you tell us more about commercial dog food?*
AK: More than 95 percent of US companion animals derive their nutritional needs from a single source: processed pet food. The commercial pet food industry is a very big business. Profits are achieved by minimizing the costs and maximizing the taste, smell, color, and texture of the products sold. The industry uses a variety of ingenious pet food substrates to minimize its costs, some of which may pose health hazards. Consumers are misled by advertisements displaying whole choice cuts of animal product. They are unaware that manufacturers have long since substituted

all the parts of the animal unfit for human consumption known as "byproducts," and slaughterhouse wastes. Commercial dog food may contain meat from animals that are dead, dying, diseased, or disabled on arrival at the slaughterhouse. The food may also contain supermarket rejects, and large numbers of rendered dogs and cats euthanized in animal shelters. Old restaurant grease complete with high concentrations of dangerous free radicals and trans fatty acids; PCBs, heavy metals, and other toxins, particularly from fish; bacterial, protozoal, fungal, hormone, and antibiotic residues; and dangerous preservatives are all rendered delicious to cats and dogs by the addition of "digest," a soup of partially dissolved entrails from chickens and other animals.

M&L: *How do these companies get away with this kind of food for our pets, and couldn't they do better?*

AK: It's about maximizing profits. Pet food scientists have long since learned how to fortify a mixture of otherwise inedible scraps with artificial vitamins and minerals and preserve them to resist degradation during storage for a year or longer. They extrude the resultant mixture into whimsical shapes that appeal to the human consumer.

M&L: *What are a couple of your best suggestions regarding feeding our dogs?*

AK: Two things: First, in terms of safeguarding our dogs' health, their nutritional needs come first. They need a complete and balanced diet. Meat diets do not meet the nutritional needs of dogs. They need a combination of live organic bioavailable vegetables, protein, and supplementation. Second, monitor the acidity of their urine; if it becomes alkaline, then it can be corrected with foods. You can check your dog's urine at your veterinarian or purchase a dog and cat urine test kit at your pharmacy.

M&L: *What is the best way to transition a dog to a vegan diet?*

AK: Transitioning is very important. It should be done very gradually so that digestion and intestinal flora can have time to transition. You could start with 10 percent new food mixed into their regular meal for a few days. Then move to 20 percent for a few more days. Move on in this manner until you are feeding a 100 percent plant-based diet.

Steve Brown

One of our luckiest finds is Steve Brown. Steve is a renowned dog nutrition expert who has been in the raw dog food industry since its start. He's been called the Godfather of Raw Dog Food by many (raw, as in raw meat), but is most known for his books, *Unlocking the Canine Ancestral Diet* and *See Spot Live Longer*. Steve has appeared in many documentaries talking about complete and balanced food for dogs.

Why would we go to someone who is an expert in what is called the ancestral diet for dogs, which is basically what wolves ate in the wild? Well, we wanted to know why this diet was supposed to be good for our dogs and if a vegan diet could live up to keeping our dogs healthy and thriving.

Steve Brown is not normally a promoter of vegan or vegetarian diets for dogs, but when we contacted him, he understood our mission to bring the healthiest vegan diet to vegan parents. We think he was very curious and decided to work with us. Steve has invented a Dog Food Formulation Chart. It's digital. You put in an ingredient and the amount you are serving and it tells you if it has everything your dog needs for a healthy diet. After he ran a few of our recipes through his chart, we think he was surprised with how well a vegan diet could work. We decided to continue our relationship and work with him further to help formulate the best plant-based diet that is complete and balanced.

Mimi and Lisa: *Can you tell us about the ancestral diet for dogs?*
Steve Brown: Our dog ancestors, the wolves, were always aware of the possibility of starving to death, so they overlooked no food. Our present dogs are not the same. My dogs have probably never worried about starving to death.

M&L: *How was the wolf's diet balanced?*
SB: About 49 percent of the calories were from protein, 45 percent from fat, and 6 percent from carbohydrates. The ancestral diet contained roughage and non-digestible parts, had a high mineral content, and, unlike kibble, a full range of vitamins and antioxidants. The protein and fat content is a yearly average. Even the fattiest prey in the best of years had a lot less fat than do our feedlot-fed animals today.

Feeding a dog, a domesticated animal, compared to a wild animal, is not the same.

Let's take manganese. Manganese is a trace mineral important to a healthy body. It supports the bones, kidneys, and pancreas, just to name a few benefits. Wolves in the wild would obtain 100 percent manganese from their diet whereas domestic animals have 50 percent less in today's diet.

M&L: *Is it possible to feed a dog a vegan diet and complete all their nutritional needs?*
SB: If every nutritional need is met, it's possible. There are so many things to take into consideration even when feeding a dog a standard diet. Each nutrient completes another.

M&L: *What is your opinion on what we are doing to bring vegan recipes to vegan dog parents who don't want to give their dogs parts of other animals?*
SB: My consent to work with you is based on the knowledge that vegans will feed their dogs vegan food. Like you, I want dogs to live long, healthy lives. I would rather see a book that is formulated and thought out than just someone haphazardly feeding their dog vegan meals that are lacking in nutrients.

DOGGIE HISTORY AND THE GREAT DOMESTICATION DEBATE

Studies say man's best friend may have been domesticated somewhere around 15,000 to 33,000 years ago, evolving from wolves. Dogs have been around a long time and are the first domesticated animal, so you can imagine how they became our companions.

Although related to wolves, dogs have changed in temperament and body. Their skulls and teeth shrank and their paws became smaller. They became more docile, friendlier, and more sensitive to human energies and feelings. Dogs have changed from wild wolves to modern pooches that have been crossbred so often with each other's genes that they are completely homogenized. Many dog breeders choose to maintain the purity of breeds that are centuries old and do not crossbreed.

The domestication of dogs over time, in some ways, created a new animal distant from the wolf. Dogs are more sensitive to human hand cues. They learn commands such as "Get your leash," and they retrieve the leash. They play Frisbee and retrieve their ball or toy. They can feel our emotions when we arrive home from a hard day. Dogs are known to have different barks to express themselves for different emotions. Wolves make different sounds. We often see commercials for dog food comparing a domesticated dog to a wolf when it comes to nutrition, but how similar are they? Even if there are signs of DNA from the wolf era, it does not comprise the whole dog of today. What we need to remember is that wolves are wild animals. They have scavenger tendencies and are always hunting for food. A domesticated dog is part of a healthy household and they know that their food will be provided for them. Any attempt to compare the nutritional needs of a wild animal to a domesticated dog of today might be unjust to both of their unique experiences.

CHAPTER TWO

Preparing Plant-Based Dog Food

———o———

COMPLETE AND BALANCED—INCLUDING SUPPLEMENTATION

So what does complete and balanced mean? This is not a one-size-fits-all subject.

Dogs at different ages have different nutritional requirements. Our recipes are formulated for adult dogs, but puppies have a different set of needs. The Vegan Dog Nutrition Association and the AAFCO (Association of American Feed Control Officials) recommend balancing 18 percent to 22 percent of your dog's meal with a protein source. A dog's protein requirements are greater than human needs. Protein requirements may be satisfied with well-cooked legumes, including pinto beans—which are the most non-allergenic food for dogs—lentils, garbanzo beans, buckwheat, quinoa, hemp, and our SuperBoost (see page 144)

There are twenty-three amino acids and ten of those are essential, meaning that a dog must obtain them through food. This is not to suggest that the others are not significant, but a dog can manufacture them from the essential ten. Balancing calcium and phosphorus ratios is another important element, and sometimes supplements are needed.

The remaining part of your dog's meal can be made up of a variety of raw and cooked vegetables. Orange and yellow vegetables, including sweet potatoes, carrots, yellow sweet pepper, and squash, are important sources of beta-carotene and should be included in your dog's food on a regular basis. Dogs convert beta-carotene into Vitamin A, which is a necessary and important nutrient.

Our recipes contain vitamins and minerals, including zinc—which is an important trace mineral and can be found in pumpkin seeds, wheat germ, sesame seeds, and chickpeas.

Selenium, a mineral that has antioxidant properties, is great for skin and coat. Selenium strengthens the immune system and helps with proper thyroid function. Brazil nuts and spinach are foods with high selenium content and we have included these in our recipes and SuperSeedDust (see page 144).

Spinach, sweet potato, wheat germ, sunflower seeds, and butternut squash are loaded with vitamin E and you will find these important foods in our recipes.

Other vegetables, some raw and some cooked, including broccoli, Brussels sprouts, sea vegetables, and dark leafy greens, supply enzymes, fiber, vitamins, and minerals. We use vegetables containing phytonutrients and antioxidants, which help support a healthy urinary tract, as well as dental and heart health.

We include recipes for what we call SuperDusts and SuperBoosts. They are combinations of superfoods, minerals, green leafy vegetables, and spirulina. Our dusts and boosts include other highly nutritious plant foods, making it easy to prepare them ahead and have on hand to sprinkle on your dog's food for added nutrients. Adding a sprinkle of sea vegetables such as kelp or dulse helps to supply a source of minerals.

Our SuperYeastDust is a rich source of vitamin B12. Our recipes also contain flaxseed meal, hemp, and coconut oil, which are good for coat, skin, and healthy joint function. You can see a noticeable difference in your dog's coat when including the right oils in their diet. These oils contain the essential fatty acids omega-3, -6, and -9, which can deliver improvement to your dog's joints, especially in senior dogs. Just a drizzle over your dog's food will put pep in their step.

Some fruits are good for dogs

We recommend blueberries, strawberries, and blackberries, which are very high in antioxidants. Bananas, apples (seeds removed, as apple seeds are toxic for dogs), and watermelon (seeds removed) are safe fruits for your dog as well. Fruits should always be served without protein foods as the enzymes and sugars could cause digestive discomfort. Fruits are a treat and contain natural sugars.

We believe in organic, non-GMO foods

We choose not to use soy products in our recipes, such as tofu. Many dogs can be allergic to soy and most soy products are GMO. We also do not include seitan (a "wheat-meat"), which is made from gluten flour.

Allergies can disappear on a plant-based diet

Some dogs may have allergies, which could go away after being on a plant-based diet. It's a good idea to have blood work done the first three to six months after transitioning to assure there are no allergies or deficiencies. You should also have their urine pH tested or test yourself with Solid Gold Pet pH testing strips, found at your pharmacy. Dog urine should be between the 6.5 and 7 range. If it's not acidic enough, you can supplement with Cranimals or chop fresh or frozen cranberries into their food.

Every dog breed can have specific needs. We suggest you do extensive research for your particular breed. Stay open to new findings and research just as you do for your own health. As in humans, fruits and vegetables are the cornerstone of a healthy body. In commercial dog food, you will find very little of these fresh items. Free radicals destroy cells in both humans and dogs and without fruits and vegetables that contain rich antioxidants, minerals, and vitamins, the body can expect these free radicals to take over. Loss of cells means disease and a shorter lifespan. Phytochemicals and antioxidants in fruits and vegetables can prevent arthritic pain and help to preserve and strengthen DNA. See our A–Z Glossary Unleashed (page 153) for complete nutritional value of individual fruits and vegetables.

What transformations will you notice?

Change in diet takes time to notice, but we've read stories and talked to pet parents who claim their dog's temperament changed after eating a plant-based diet and their aggressive behavior turned more gentle. Their dog would normally chase after small animals such as rabbits and squirrels, but once on a plant-based diet, they started protecting and playing with these small wild animals.

Dogs on plant-based diets have made remarkable transformations in their physical health and their temperaments. Many vegan pet families say they have even felt more closeness from their dog.

What if I still want to feed my dog meat?

Of course you have the choice to continue to feed your dog meat, but they still need vegetables, fruits, herbs, and superfoods. Meat alone or processed commercial foods will not supply your dog all the nutrients they need to stay healthy. We suggest you add fresh plant food to your dog's current diet and follow the same transitioning plan. We encourage a plant-based, compassionate diet for humans and dogs.

Why are your recipes so delicious?

We've created recipes that you can eat as well as feed to your dog. All you have to do is separate out your dog's portion and add some more seasonings that might not be dog-friendly to your portion. We know, it sounds funny to be eating dog food, but since it's human grade, organic, delicious, and healthy, why not?

For example, take our recipe for Veggie Tagine: Add additional Moroccan spices

to your portion and this might become a family favorite—and your dog's favorite as well. Our cracker treats are so delicious, it will be hard to keep your hand out of their doggie treat jar, but, again, that's okay. And who knows, it might be healthier than your regular diet. With common kitchen tools and some guidance, you will know exactly what's going into your dog's food.

Balance is obtained over time and not necessarily in each meal. This is why variety is the key. As long as your dog gets everything they need spread out within the week, their diet will be complete and balanced. You will find nutritional value of foods we use in our recipes in our A–Z Glossary Unleashed (page 153).

Supplementation

Having said all this, each dog is different in breed, digestion, exercise lifestyle, previous illness, and disease. The best way to know if your dog is getting the proper nutrition is to see your veterinarian and have your dog take a blood test approximately three to six months after transitioning. This will show if your dog is lacking in any particular vitamin. Our recipes have the nutrients your dog needs, but since no two dogs are alike, you could have one dog that needs more calcium while your other dog is fine, even though they are eating the same meal. The same goes for humans. Two people in the same household can consume the same food and still have different nutritional needs. You can purchase an organic head of broccoli from one grower and another head from a different grower and they could both show up with different nutritional values. Soil condition, water, and other factors come into play, so blood testing for your dog is very important. The same goes for you. Taking supplements without having your blood tested to see what you need is just guesswork. Some dogs might need a multivitamin or supplement of taurine or calcium added to their diet.

Taurine is an amino acid naturally found in animal protein, but not in plants. A deficiency can be very serious, especially with certain breeds, so a supplement might be recommended. Taurine can be ordered online or purchased at your local health food store. You can use human-grade supplements. Check with your veterinarian for dosage.

Vitamin B12 is included in our recipes in the form of nutritional yeast, but some dogs might need more supplementation of B12 or may be allergic to yeast. In this case, a multivitamin is recommended.

Vitamin D is another requirement for a healthy dog, but, if given too much, it may be toxic. Again, we stress to check with your veterinarian before giving your dog any supplements. We use spirulina in our recipes and implore you to do your research and purchase a high-quality product. There are a lot of brands available on the market, but not all of them are pure. Some can have high levels of heavy metal or can be contaminated. Do your due diligence and find out how the manufacturer sources their product. One brand we recommend is Earthrise, which can be purchased online or at your local health food store.

If your veterinarian informs you that your dog needs more calcium, we recommend Animals Essentials Calcium, which is derived from seaweed. See label for recommended dose. It can be purchased online at Amazon or Chewy.com.

For optimum urinary tract health, a product called Cranimals is an antioxidant supplement made from organic cranberries. See label for suggested serving. This product can be purchased online or at Amazon.

An all-around supplement source worth looking into is Vegedog and is available at www.compassioncircle.com.

With all supplementation, we recommend you speak with your veterinarian, especially if your dog is on any medication, as some supplementation might interfere with their current medications.

ABOUT OUR RECIPES

Recipes are made with fresh, organic, colorful vegetables and fruits. They contain beans and rice, superfoods, seeds, healthy oils, sea vegetables, and herbs. A dog's digestive tract is shorter than ours, so they cannot digest large chunks of food. We shred, grate, puree, or finely chop all our meals. Some items are served raw and others cooked. Meals are served at room temperature or slightly warmed. We recommend always having filtered water in a clean bowl available for your dog. On page 141, you will also find infused water ideas, which will encourage your dog to drink more water for proper hydration.

How to cook and store the basics

The basics are ingredients that you will use as a daily base in your dog's bowl. A base might include lentils, beans, quinoa, buckwheat, or wild rice. To save time, make it ahead and refrigerate it for a few days or freeze it for longer periods. You will find cooking instructions on page 52.

How to use SuperBoost and SuperDusts

Our SuperBoost and SuperDusts are important additions to a meal. We include them in the recipes not as an option but as a necessity for balanced nutrition. Please add where the recipe calls for them. You might be temped to give your dog more Superfoods than recommended, but more is not necessarily better. Please use the amount we suggest.

Toxic food for dogs

It is important to know what your dog should NOT eat as well as what they should eat. Many lists say different things regarding toxic food for dogs. We have researched and worked with veterinarians to determine which are in fact toxic. When disposing of any of these foods, be sure your dog does not get into the garbage and accidentally consume these items. Also, it is extremely important to read all packaged products, including supplements, before giving them to your dog. Often there are hidden ingredients. If there is an ingredient you are not familiar with, always do the research to confirm it is safe for dogs.

Added salt	Grapes
Alcohol	Nutmeg
Apple seeds and stem	Nuts
Avocados	Onion
Caffeine	Persimmons
Candy	Pits from any stone fruit
Chips	Raisins
Chocolate	Spring Parsley
Citrus	Xylitol (an artificial sweetener that
Cocoa Powder	is toxic for dogs, which sometimes
Coffee	may be hidden in peanut butter)
Garlic	

For busy people: how to prepare a week's worth of meals in advance

Prepare the basics and store each portion in airtight glass containers according to your dog's weight (page 49). Basics should be approximately two-thirds of your dog's meal. You can mix and match basics if desired, as long as they are of similar value. Cooked and fresh raw vegetables should be the remaining one-third of your dog's meal. Sprinkle Boosts, Dusts, and toppings on your dog's food to assure a balanced meal.

To prepare a stored meal, remove the basic from the refrigerator and assemble the additional cooked and raw food to the base. Rather than reheat the base, it's best to add a few tablespoons of warm water or Calcium Broth (page 113) and mix it in. Mash ingredients together with a fork and break it down to bite-size texture. Always follow the recipe for added toppings. These are not options, but necessary for a balanced meal.

WHAT YOU WILL NEED

Pantry staples

Pantry staples will simplify preparing homemade meals. If you have all the base ingredients on hand, then all you have left to do is shop weekly for the fresh ingredients.

Amaranth

Apple cider vinegar

Barley

Beans (garbanzo, pinto, black, kidney, cannellini)

Brown rice

Buckwheat

Chia seeds

Coconut oil

Cranberries (frozen)

Filtered water

Flaxseed meal (you can grind flaxseeds to make it into meal)

Flaxseed oil

Gluten-free oats

Gluten-free pasta

Hemp hearts

Hemp seed oil

Kelp or dulse

Lentils

Nutritional yeast

Peas (frozen)

Pumpkin seeds

Quinoa

Spirulina (use a high-quality brand; see page 43 under *Supplementation*)

Sunflower seeds

Tahini

Turmeric

Wheat germ

Wild rice

Kitchen Essentials & Simple Tools

You probably have all you need in your kitchen if you cook your own meals, but there may be a few small tools that will make preparing your dog's food easier and more fun. If you do not have some of these items on hand, just improvise. Not everyone likes to cook, so the idea of cooking for your dog might not seem appealing, but love always wins, and since we are sure you love your companion and are happy when they're happy, we think you'll find preparing homemade food for your dog enjoyable. The fact that you're this far along in the book tells us you are committed to helping your dog live a long, healthy life.

Chopping board

Dehydrator (optional, but really
    helpful for treats)

Food processor or blender

Glass jars and containers with
    airtight lids

Microplane grater

Sharp chopping knife

Spiralizer or potato peeler

Ziplock freezer bags

When preparing vegetables, a sharp chopping knife is always important. A chopping board is advisable as it makes it easier to chop properly.

A food processor is a real help for quickly chopping food to its desired consistency. Most dogs just gulp their food down without chewing, so breaking their food up into small pieces is essential.

A box or microplane grater is another handy tool. This is used for shredding things such as carrots, zucchini, and other raw foods for topping your dog's meal. A grater is especially handy if you're feeding your dog standard dry kibble or processed food, as it allows you to quickly add fresh vegetables. Remember: Your dog needs fresh foods for proper digestion and ultimate health.

A dehydrator is not a must, as an oven can do the job, but it's useful to make Sweet Potato Chews, Canine Crackers, and SuperKaleDust. A dehydrator can save you money, as extra veggies can be chopped and dehydrated to reconstitute at a later time to quickly add to your dog's meal. Another plus for a dehydrator is that the food is considered raw if the temperature is set to 118°F or less. This retains the nutrients and enzymes. With a dehydrator, you can turn it on and not worry about watching the time as there is no burning involved. You can find an inexpensive one or buy a nicer brand such as the Excalibur, which you can use to make other family treats. If you don't have a dehydrator, you can use an oven set on the lowest temperature. Just check in to make sure the food is drying out properly and not burning.

Storage containers are helpful for making large-batch meals. You can store them in the freezer for up to a month, or hold them in the refrigerator for up to 3 days. Glass containers with airtight lids are recommended, as it's the healthiest way to freeze and store food, but ziplock–style bags will work for convenience, as well.

HOW TO TRANSITION YOUR DOG

Transitioning your dog is very important and it's better to go slowly. To transition your dog to a plant-based diet, start by using 90 percent of their regular food with 10 percent of their new food. Do this for three days, then move to adding 20 percent for a few more days. Continue this process until you're feeding 100 percent plant-based food. If your dog seems sensitive to new foods, you can follow this percent ratio every time you introduce a new food combination.

In order to avoid any digestive disorders when transitioning, see how your dog adjusts after the first three days. Take a full week or longer if necessary before increasing the percentage, especially if your dog is used to an animal-based diet. (Younger dogs seem to transition more quickly.) Often, once your dog knows how delicious the food is, they adjust quickly and look forward to their meal. We've seen dogs newly introduced to a plant-based meal that can't stop licking their bowl for remaining specks.

If you feed your dog once a day, it's a good idea, when transitioning to a plant-based diet, to feed them two smaller meals daily plus a couple of our healthy snack recipes. If your dog turns up their nose the first time you feed them a new diet, remember that dogs smell first before tasting: Add some of their favorite food to each meal. Keep in mind that homemade plant-based food can heal disease and keep your dog fit.

How Much Should You Feed Your Dog?

As many as half of all dogs are overweight, according to the Association for Pet Obesity Prevention. A number of reasons could factor into this: processed commercial food, inadequate exercise, and, less mysteriously, overeating. Dogs love to eat, so sometimes we give them more food than they need, because we love them and want to see them happy. The good news is that very often, feeding your dog a fresh food diet allows excess weight to drop off naturally. Feeding fresh treats in between meals such as blueberries, slices of apple or carrot, or dehydrated sweet potato are a much healthier alternative for your dog than a processed, store-bought snack.

Like overweight humans, overweight dogs are more susceptible to diseases. Finding and maintaining your dog's weight can extend their life. It's not as easy as feeding your dog less food when they are overweight. It can depend on each dog's activity level as well as age and breed. Your veterinarian can help you with determining your dog's proper weight but, as a general rule, adult dogs will eat around 2 to 3 percent of their body weight in fresh food daily. Plant-based foods tend to be lower in calories, so you might need to adjust according to your dog's activity level. While feeding your dog a plant-based fresh food diet, what you might find is that your dog will naturally adjust to their proper weight. A dog that is lean lives longer and healthier.

GENERAL FEEDING CHART FOR ADULT DOGS

DOG SIZE	MEAL SIZE
Toy breeds and small-breed dogs weighing fewer than 10 pounds	Feed approximately ¼ to ½ cup per meal, twice per day
Miniature and small-breed dogs weighing 10 to 15 pounds	Feed approximately ½ to 1 cup per meal, twice per day
Medium-breed dogs weighing 25 to 50 pounds	Feed approximately 1 to 2 cups per meal, twice per day
Large-breed dogs weighing 50 to 75 pounds	Feed approximately 2 to 3 cups per meal, twice per day
Extra-large breed dogs weighing over 75 pounds	Feed approximately 3 to 4 cups per meal, twice per day

CHAPTER THREE

Recipes for Plant-Based Dog Food
MAIN MEAL DOG BOWLS

———o———

THERE ARE A VARIETY OF RECIPES FOR YOUR DOG'S MAIN BOWL MEAL. PICKING a selection of two different recipes weekly and alternating during the week works well. Follow recipes as suggested, including toppings and superfoods, as they have been formulated for a complete and balanced meal.

Portion out from each recipe the amount your dog eats in one meal. The remainder can be refrigerated for another meal or frozen for a later time. Be sure to mark the date on the leftover storage container. Most meals are best consumed refrigerated in 2 to 3 days or up to 1 month if frozen.

HOW TO MAKE THE BASICS

It's important to cook basics and have them on hand for daily meals. Having them ready to go makes preparing meals quick and easy. Review the recipes you plan on making that week and prepare basics for these meals. This is a great time-saver.

Once you've made your batch of basics, portion out what you will need for a few days and refrigerate. The rest can be portioned into single servings in airtight glass containers or ziplock bags. Place the date on the container and freeze. When ready to use, defrost in the refrigerator overnight. Place food into your dog's bowl, add warm water or calcium broth, the fresh portion of the meal, some toppings and superfood. Lightly toss and you have a meal in just a few minutes.

One or more of the basics are usually served each meal. Our methods for cooking are stovetop, but a rice cooker can also be used for grains. Please do not use a microwave.

Amaranth: Combine 2½ to 3 cups filtered water to 1 cup amaranth in a pot and bring to a boil. Let boil for 2 minutes, cover, reduce heat, and simmer for 20 to 30 minutes or until grains are fluffy and water is absorbed. The more water, the softer the amaranth.

Beans (including black, navy, kidney, pinto, cannellini, mung, and garbanzo): Pick through beans, removing any shriveled or foreign matter. One pound of dry beans makes approximately 5 to 6 cups cooked beans. Rinse beans well, place in a pot, and cover with cold water. Leave the beans to soak overnight, then drain and rinse beans. In a large pot, add fresh filtered water and beans. For each cup of beans, add 5 cups of filtered water. Bring to a boil for 2 to 3 minutes and turn down heat to a very low simmer. Most beans will cook in 1 to 2 hours. Check beans occasionally to see if more water is needed. To test for doneness, mash one bean on the side of the pot with a fork or spoon, or taste a bean. SuperHerbDust (page 145) may be added to the pot when the beans are tender. Adding this herb mix before they are tender could toughen the beans. Refrigerate in an airtight glass container or ziplock bag for up to 3 days or freeze for up to a month.

TIPS: Help reduce gas production by changing the soaking water once or twice. Also, adding a 1-inch piece of kombu seaweed will help with gas as well. If using container or canned beans, make sure there are not any hidden ingredients and always rinse in a strainer over the sink with running cold water.

Buckwheat: Wash 1 cup buckwheat groats in a bowl. Pour into a strainer and rinse over the sink. Drain well. In a medium saucepan, combine 1¾ cups filtered water and the buckwheat. Bring to a simmer and put the lid on. Simmer on low for 18 to 20 minutes. Shut off heat and let sit 5 to 10 minutes. Refrigerate in an airtight glass container or ziplock bag for up to 3 days or freeze for up to a month.

Lentils: Rinse 1 cup lentils in a strainer over the sink. Drain well. Add 3 cups of filtered water to the pot and add lentils. Cook on the stovetop in a large pot. Lentils swell when cooked. Bring water to a boil, then turn down heat and simmer. Put on a tight-fitting lid and simmer for approximately 20 to 25 minutes, or until tender. Refrigerate in an airtight glass container or ziplock bag for up to 3 days or freeze for up to a month.

Rice, Brown: Place 1 cup brown rice in a strainer and rinse in the sink under cold running water. Bring 2¼ cups filtered water to a boil and add brown rice. When water boils, cover pot and reduce to a low simmer. Cook 45 minutes with the lid on. Do not open pot and let steam out. Turn off flame and let sit 15 minutes without lifting lid. Fluff with a fork. Refrigerate in an airtight glass container or ziplock bag for up to 3 days or freeze for up to a month.

Rice, Wild: Place 1 cup wild rice in a strainer and rinse in the sink under cold running water. Bring rice and 4 cups filtered water to a boil. Reduce to a low simmer and put the lid on. Cook 45 to 50 minutes, or until grains are tender. Let rice steam with the heat off and lid on for 15 minutes. Fluff with a fork when ready and store in an airtight glass container. Refrigerate in an airtight glass container or ziplock bag for up to 3 days or freeze for up to a month.

Quinoa: It's best for digestion to soak quinoa overnight, then strain and rinse over the sink with running water. Place 2 cups filtered water and 1 cup rinsed and soaked quinoa in a pot and bring to a boil for 2 minutes. Turn the heat down and simmer. Put a tight-fitting lid on and cook until the water is absorbed, about 15 minutes. Taste for doneness. Refrigerate in an airtight glass container or ziplock bag for up to 3 days or freeze for up to a month. The best way to obtain all the benefits from quinoa is to soak and sprout the hulled grain. This helps unleash the nutrients so your dog can absorb and use the vitamins found in the grain.

DOG BOWLS

Your dog's bowl may be part of your kitchen or at least part of your home. You will notice in our photos that meals are served in attractive bowls. It's not just due to a photo shoot for the book, but points to our foodie obsession. We know Fido won't care—but why not make their serving bowl look good just for the love of it or for your adoring Instagram followers?

The beauty of your dog's bowl is one thing, but the material your dog's bowl is made of can impact their health. It's a good idea to check their bowls often and replace them if cracked. Always wash your dog's bowl with hot, soapy water before serving their meal. A clean bowl at each meal ensures that no bacteria can accumulate.

Plastic bowls can easily be scratched, making them a breeding ground for bacteria. They can also leach BPA and can be dangerous if your dog chews on their bowl.

Stainless-steel bowls don't collect bacteria if they're kept clean. They are easy to wash and are unbreakable.

Look for lead-free ceramic or glass bowls, which are easy to clean and look attractive. Our very favorite gorgeous bowls are from PawNosh. Skilled glassmakers with the highest craftsmanship forge these bowls, which are made in the USA from recycled glass (www.pawnosh.com).

GRAIN-FREE OVERNIGHT BREAKFAST BOWL

When you add liquid to chia seeds and let them soak overnight, they become gelatinous and almost like a pudding. Chia seeds contain protein and omega-3 fatty acids, which are also found in wheat germ. Adding chia seeds to your dog's diet can help fight allergies, relieve itchy skin, and boost their immune system. Use a spoonful or two as a treat, or mixed into cooked quinoa for a light breakfast.

MAKES 1 SERVING

1 teaspoon hemp seeds

1 teaspoon chia seeds

¼ teaspoon flaxseed meal

¼ teaspoon wheat germ

¼ cup coconut water or filtered water

TOPPING

Berries

Diced bananas

DIRECTIONS

Combine hemp seeds, chia seeds, flaxseed meal, and wheat germ with coconut water. Let sit out 10 minutes and stir again. Cover with airtight lid and refrigerate overnight.

TO SERVE

When ready to serve, remove from the refrigerator and add warm filtered water to desired consistency. Place proper portion for your dog in feeding bowl (see Feeding Chart on page 49). Top with berries and diced bananas and stir. Store in an airtight glass container or ziplock bag in the refrigerator for up to 3 days or freeze for up to 1 month.

OATMEAL BLAST BREAKFAST BOWL

This is a great way for your dog (and you) to start the day. Add in fresh berries, banana, and sprinkle with pumpkin seeds for a power-packed meal. Make oatmeal ahead of time and reheat with warm water.

MAKES 1 CUP

1 cup cooked steel-cut oats or gluten-free oats

1 teaspoon wheat germ

1 teaspoon sunflower seed or peanut butter

1 tablespoon shaved apple

¼ teaspoon flaxseed or hemp oil

TOPPING

Sprinkle of SuperBoost (page 144)

DIRECTIONS

In a mixing bowl, combine the oats, wheat germ, sunflower seed butter, apple, and flaxseed oil. Lightly mix.

TO SERVE

Place proper portion for your dog in feeding bowl (see Feeding Chart on page 49). Top with SuperBoost. Store in an airtight glass container or ziplock bag in the refrigerator for up to 2 days.

VEGGIE TAGINE

Tagine is a traditional Moroccan clay cooking pot, which enhances the flavor and requires no oil for cooking. This recipe uses an array of colorful vegetables. The turmeric and ginger add anti-inflammatory properties. This is a dinner you can share with your dog. Just add a little bit of spicy harissa to your portion for an extra punch of flavor. Note: A cast-iron skillet with a lid can be used instead of a tagine.

MAKES 4 CUPS

¼ teaspoon turmeric

¼ teaspoon grated fresh ginger

¾ cup filtered water or broth

1 sweet potato, peeled and diced small

1 cup cooked chickpeas

1 zucchini, roughly peeled and diced small

½ cup small-diced red bell pepper

½ cup fresh or frozen peas

¼ to ½ cup cooked quinoa or couscous, for serving

TOPPING

1 tablespoon chopped fresh cilantro, mint, or sunflower sprouts

SuperSeedDust (page 144) and Super-YeastDust (page 145):

- ⅛ teaspoon of each dust for dogs up to 10 pounds
- ¼ teaspoon of each dust for dogs 20 to 40 pounds
- ½ teaspoon of each dust for dogs 50 to 80 pounds

DIRECTIONS

Add turmeric, ginger, and water to a tagine or Dutch oven with lid and stir on low heat until ginger and turmeric dissolve. Add sweet potato and let simmer about 10 to 15 minutes until tender. Add chickpeas and zucchini and simmer 3 to 5 minutes. Add a little more water if needed. Add bell pepper and peas and simmer a few more minutes until soft.

TO SERVE

Place proper portion of quinoa or couscous and vegetables for your dog in feeding bowl (see Feeding Chart on page 49). Top with fresh cilantro or alternative. Sprinkle with SuperSeedDust and SuperYeastDust. Lightly mix and serve. Store in an airtight glass container or ziplock bag in the refrigerator for up to 3 days or freeze for up to 1 month.

MEDITERRANEAN BOWL

Lentils, quinoa, and chickpeas are a great source of protein. All the vegetables in this recipe are adding cancer-fighting properties to your dog's diet. Basil may alleviate arthritis. It is also a natural insect repellent—adding a little of this fresh-chopped herb to your dog's diet can help deter fleas.

MAKES 4 CUPS

1 cup cooked lentils

1 cup cooked quinoa

1 cup finely chopped kale or spinach

½ cup small-diced red bell pepper

½ cucumber, diced small

1 carrot, grated

1 teaspoon finely chopped fresh basil

TOPPING

1 teaspoon chickpeas or Chickpea Hummus (recipe follows)

SuperSeedDust (page 144) and Super-YeastDust (page 145):

- ⅛ teaspoon of each dust for dogs up to 10 pounds
- ¼ teaspoon of each dust for dogs 20 to 40 pounds
- ½ teaspoon of each dust for dogs 50 to 80 pounds

DIRECTIONS

In a large bowl, mix lentils, quinoa, kale or spinach, red pepper, cucumber, carrot, and basil. Lightly toss.

TO SERVE

Place proper portion of chickpea or hummus for your dog in feeding bowl (see Feeding Chart on page 49). Sprinkle with SuperSeedDust and SuperYeastDust. Lightly mix and serve. Store in an airtight glass container or ziplock bag in the refrigerator for up to 3 days or freeze for up to 1 month.

CHICKPEA HUMMUS

There are so many good things about chickpeas, also known as garbanzo beans. Not only will your dog love the taste, but chickpeas are also rich in protein, magnesium, potassium, and B and C vitamins that help build the immune system. Do not feed store-bought hummus to your dog as it can contain ingredients such as garlic and onion that are toxic to dogs. If using canned beans, buy unsalted or rinse very well. Chickpea Hummus can be added to a main meal or eaten as a snack with a chopped vegetable such as carrot or zucchini.

MAKES 1 CUP

1 cup cooked chickpeas

⅓ cup raw tahini

½ teaspoon dulse

½ teaspoon turmeric

Add water a tablespoon at a time until desired consistency

DIRECTIONS

Combine all ingredients in food processor and blend until smooth and creamy.

TO SERVE

Can be added to main meals or served as a snack with finely chopped veggies.

Store in an airtight glass container or ziplock bag in the refrigerator for up to 1 week.

KRISTA AND NIGEL AND THEIR RESCUE DOGS

Krista Hiddema is Vice President of Mercy For Animals, Canada
Nigel Osborne is Executive Director of EggTruth.com

My wife and I have been rescuing dogs, including Great Danes, for many years. As long-time vegans, we ensure we adhere to a "do no harm" philosophy to every measure that is practically possible. The abundance of high-quality, nutritionally optimal, plant-based dog food allows us to extend our compassionate lifestyle to our rescues. Every time we bring in a new dog, they usually suffer from a variety of maladies and, occasionally, behavioral issues. But there is a simple remedy to this: love, exercise, and a good diet. Give them the best of all three and you'll literally transform these wonderful companions into superstars! Many visitors to our home get the opportunity to meet the "before and after" versions of the dogs we rescue. Our friends and family never fail to be shocked, and a little impressed, whenever they return for a visit and can see the transformation of the dogs over time. All that said, we do consult with our vet and have also consulted with canine nutritionists in the past for that extra bit of reassurance. As a result, we have been feeding our dogs plant-based dog food for years (with no supplements) and they maintain a healthy weight, activity level, and a disposition to match. And the nice thing is, no other animals are harmed in their rehabilitation.

VEGGIE NOODLES
WITH PEANUT SAUCE BOWL

Mung beans have been used in Ayurvedic diets for thousands of years. They offer a great source of nutrients for your dog, including a variety of minerals, vitamin B, and fiber—plus they are high in protein.

MAKES 4 CUPS

1 zucchini, roughly peeled

1 small sweet potato, roughly peeled

½ teaspoon organic coconut oil

1 cup cooked mung beans

1 cup cooked quinoa or brown rice

DRESSING

MAKES 1 SERVING

1 teaspoon unsalted sunflower butter or peanut butter

¼ teaspoon kelp

⅛ teaspoon SuperYeastDust (page 145)

2 teaspoons filtered water

DIRECTIONS

Spiralize or use a potato peeler to make zucchini and sweet potato into noodles. Dice noodles into bite-size pieces and toss them together in a bowl. In a medium sauté pan over medium heat, add coconut oil and sauté the vegetables until slightly soft. Add mung beans and quinoa or brown rice to the pan and warm. In a separate small bowl, whisk together sunflower or peanut butter, kelp, SuperYeastDust, and water until smooth and set aside.

TO SERVE

Place proper portion for your dog in feeding bowl and stir in dressing (see Feeding Chart on page 49). Store in an airtight glass container or ziplock bag in the refrigerator for up to 3 days or freeze for up to 1 month.

PASTA BY THE POOL

Your dog will love this gluten-free vegetable pasta. Amaranth is considered a seed and, along with white beans, it's full of protein. Zucchini is loaded with vitamins and minerals and considered an anti-inflammatory vegetable. Small amounts of freshly chopped basil can help deter fleas and mosquitoes.

MAKES 3 CUPS

1 zucchini, roughly peeled

2 teaspoons filtered water

3 button mushrooms, finely diced

½ red bell pepper, finely diced

1 cup cooked, mashed white beans

1 cup cooked amaranth or buckwheat

TOPPING

1 tablespoon chopped fresh basil

½ teaspoon olive oil

SuperYeastDust (page 145)

- ⅛ teaspoon of dust for dogs up to 10 pounds
- ¼ teaspoon of dust for dogs 20 to 40 pounds
- ½ teaspoon of dust for dogs 50 to 80 pounds

DIRECTIONS

Spiralize zucchini and cut into small bites, or use a potato peeler to make thin strips and chop into smaller pieces. Add water to a medium pan over medium heat and lightly sauté zucchini, mushrooms, and red bell pepper. Add mashed beans and amaranth or buckwheat and gently warm.

TO SERVE

Place proper portion for your dog in feeding bowl (see Feeding Chart on page 49), and add chopped basil, olive oil, and SuperYeastDust. Stir together. Store in an airtight glass container or ziplock bag in the refrigerator for up to 3 days or freeze for up to 1 month.

LENTILS AND CRANBERRY QUINOA

Cranberries can boost the immune system and help with your dog's urinary health. Plant-based dogs should have their urine pH checked regularly. If your dog's urine is not acidic enough, incorporating cranberry into your dog's diet can help.

MAKES 5 CUPS

1 sweet potato, peeled and cubed

1 cup finely chopped kale

½ cup diced fresh or frozen cranberries

1 zucchini, grated with microplane

1 cup cooked lentils

1 cup cooked quinoa

TOPPING

1 tablespoon chopped basil or sunflower sprouts

¼ teaspoon SuperSeedDust (page 144)

DIRECTIONS

In a medium pan over low heat, sauté sweet potato and kale until slightly tender. Add cranberries and zucchini and cook until tender. Add mixture to lentils and quinoa, and toss to combine.

TO SERVE

Place proper portion for your dog in feeding bowl (see Feeding Chart on page 49), and stir in chopped basil and SuperSeedDust. Store in an airtight glass container or ziplock bag in the refrigerator for up to 3 days or freeze for up to 1 month.

⟶⟝ TARAH MILLEN AND PEPSI ⟞⟶

Tarah Millen is a Raw Food Lifestyle Coach & YouTube Personality

Pepsi is a 7-year-old Border Collie–Australian Shepherd mix. I adopted him when he was 2 years old and he's been on a vegan diet ever since. When I transitioned him over to a plant-based diet, I noticed an improvement in his energy almost right away. Another improvement was the change in his skin and fur. Prior to eating a vegan diet, Pepsi had dandruff and also had oily, lackluster fur. This was the most drastic change I noticed, as his fur is now very soft and shiny and he has no dandruff. I feed him a vegan diet because it ensures that no harm comes to any animal. I also want to ensure that Pepsi has the least inflammatory diet possible, as he was run over by a vehicle as a puppy and had to have reconstructive surgery on his back legs and hips. He currently runs regularly and has no sign of inflammation or arthritis, which is common in aging dogs that have had reconstructive surgery. Our vet says that Pepsi is very healthy and he loves his food.

ROSEMARY VEGGIE BURGER

Pinto beans are considered one of the most non-allergenic proteins for dogs. Rosemary is a popular herb in Italian cooking and is often seen in commercial dog food as a natural preservative. A pinch of rosemary can be a source of antioxidants, promote heart health, and help with digestion. Like basil, it can also repel fleas. Avoid using rosemary or rosemary oil if your dog suffers from seizures or is pregnant.

MAKES APPROXIMATELY 12 PATTIES

1 tablespoon flaxseed meal

3 tablespoons filtered water

2 cups cooked organic pinto beans

1 tablespoon pumpkin seeds

½ cup kale, stems removed

½ handful of fresh parsley

⅓ cup grated sweet potato

½ teaspoon turmeric

½ teaspoon kelp

½ teaspoon finely chopped fresh rosemary

1 teaspoon organic coconut oil

½ cup quinoa flour

1½ cups cooked quinoa, buckwheat, or amaranth

Choice of vegetables, according to proper portions (see Note below)

TOPPING

¼ teaspoon SuperYeastDust (page 145)

DIRECTIONS

Preheat oven to 350°F and line a baking sheet with parchment paper. In a small bowl, mix flaxseed meal with water and let sit until it thickens, 5 to 7 minutes. This is known as a flax egg, which helps bind ingredients. In a food processor, add cooked pinto beans and pumpkin seeds and pulse until blended. Add kale and parsley, and lightly pulse until combined. Remove mixture to a large mixing bowl and add grated sweet potato, turmeric, kelp, rosemary, coconut oil, quinoa flour, flax mixture, and chosen grain. Combine well. Next, wet your hands and take ¼ to ½ cup, place mixture into your palms, and form into a burger. Flatten onto parchment paper. Continue making burgers, until all the mixture is used. Bake for 15 minutes, flip burgers, and bake for an additional 15 minutes. Remove from oven and let cool for 5 to 10 minutes.

continued

TO SERVE

Place proper portion of vegetables for your dog in feeding bowl (see Feeding Chart on page 49). Crumble the necessary amount of veggie burger on top of the bed of vegetables. Sprinkle on SuperYeastDust and mix in. Store in an airtight glass container or ziplock bag in the refrigerator for up to 3 days or freeze for up to 1 month. To reheat, mix portion together with a few tablespoons of warm water.

NOTE: Each serving uses a variety of fresh chopped vegetables of your choice, including chopped kale, spinach, sunflower or pea sprouts, grated carrots, finely chopped zucchini, or red bell pepper. The amount depends on the size of your dog; for example, ¼ to ⅓ cup of veggies is good for a 10-pound dog. See the Feeding Chart on page 49 for more information.

TIP: If feeding this meal for a few days, switch up the fresh raw vegetables for variety.

EASY ONE-POT MEAL

Leafy green vegetables are rich in calcium, and pea or sunflower sprouts can provide an additional boost of vitamins and protein. A small amount of freshly chopped mint can freshen your dog's breath, aid in digestion, and is known to help with seasonal allergies.

MAKES 3 CUPS

1 cup uncooked quinoa, buckwheat, or millet

2 cups filtered water

½ teaspoon organic coconut oil

¼ teaspoon turmeric

½ teaspoon SuperHerbDust (page 145)

1 cup cooked pinto beans

1 cup finely chopped leafy green vegetables

TOPPING

3 fresh mint leaves, or pea or sunflower sprouts, chopped

SuperBoost (page 144) and Super-YeastDust (page 145):

- ⅛ teaspoon of each boost/dust for dogs up to 10 pounds
- ¼ teaspoon of each boost/dust for dogs 20 to 40 pounds
- ½ teaspoon of each boost/dust for dogs 50 to 80 pounds

DIRECTIONS

Rinse grains well and place in rice cooker or pot. Add room temperature filtered water, coconut oil, turmeric, and SuperHerbDust and cook over medium heat. While grains are cooking, smash cooked beans in a bowl with a fork and set aside. About 10 to 15 minutes before grains are finished, add in the vegetables and let steam with grains until tender. Add grains and vegetables to mashed beans and mix together.

TO SERVE

Place proper portion for your dog in feeding bowl (see Feeding Chart on page 49), and top with chopped mint or sprouts, SuperBoost, and SuperYeastDust. Lightly mix and serve. Store in an airtight glass container or ziplock bag in the refrigerator for up to 3 days or freeze for up to 1 month.

BLACK BEAN BOWL

Cabbage is a cruciferous, cancer-fighting vegetable and many dogs love it. It can be eaten raw in small amounts with maximum benefits. It does contain a natural compound called thiocyanate, which, when fed in very large amounts, can suppress the thyroid. Lightly cooking it deactivates the thiocyanate.

MAKES 4 CUPS

1 sweet potato, peeled and cubed

½ cup shredded red cabbage

¼ cup filtered water

Pinch of SuperHerbDust (page 145)

1 cup cooked black beans

1 cup cooked coconut rice or quinoa (see note below)

¼ cup cucumber, peeled and diced

1 tablespoon finely chopped cilantro

TOPPING

SuperBoost (page 144) and SuperYeastDust (page 145):

- ⅛ teaspoon of each boost/dust for dogs up to 10 pounds
- ¼ teaspoon of each boost/dust for dogs 20 to 40 pounds
- ½ teaspoon of each boost/dust for dogs 50 to 80 pounds

DIRECTIONS

In a medium sauté pan over medium heat, sauté sweet potato with cabbage in water with SuperHerbDust until soft. Drain off water and place into a mixing bowl. Add beans, rice, cucumber, and cilantro.

TO SERVE

Place proper portion for your dog in feeding bowl (see Feeding Chart on page 49), and top with SuperBoost and SuperYeastDust. Store in an airtight glass container or ziplock bag in the refrigerator for up to 3 days or freeze for up to 1 month.

NOTE: To make coconut rice or quinoa, prepare as directed on page 53. While still warm, stir in 1 teaspoon coconut oil.

LENTIL CASSEROLE

Lentils are packed with protein and are high in iron as well as selenium, which can help improve the immune system and prevent inflammation. They're easy to prepare, since they do not require soaking. Cook well for easier digestion.

MAKES 6 CUPS

1½ cups dried lentils

3 cups filtered water

1 tablespoon olive oil

1 teaspoon SuperHerbDust (page 145)

1 cup chopped kale, stems removed

½ small beet, cubed

1 small sweet potato, peeled and cubed

1 cup cooked quinoa or amaranth

DRESSING

MAKES 1 SERVING

¼ teaspoon apple cider vinegar

¼ teaspoon chopped fresh parsley

⅛ teaspoon grated fresh ginger

½ teaspoon hemp seed oil

⅛ teaspoon SuperYeastDust (page 145)

DIRECTIONS

Preheat oven to 400°F. Rinse lentils well, picking out any stones, drain, and set aside. In a medium roasting pan over medium heat, add the olive oil and SuperHerbDust. Add kale, beet, and sweet potato, coating the vegetables with the oil-SuperHerbDust mixture. Cook vegetables until soft, approximately 20 minutes. Stir in the lentils and water. Cover the pan with a lid or foil and cook in the oven until lentils are tender and all water has been absorbed, approximately 50 minutes to 1 hour. Remove pan from oven and let cool. Mix in cooked quinoa or amaranth.

TO SERVE

Place proper portion for your dog in feeding bowl (see Feeding Chart on page 49). Mix all dressing ingredients together in a small bowl and drizzle over the meal. Lightly mix and serve. Store in an airtight glass container or ziplock bag in the refrigerator for up to 3 days or freeze for up to 1 month.

BUDDHA BOWL

Kale is full of important minerals and is a popular cancer-fighting vegetable. Look for organic kale and lightly steam. With any cruciferous vegetable, they can be thyroid disrupters if fed in large amounts. It is always best to use in moderation and to rotate in your dog's diet.

MAKES 3 CUPS

½ cup chopped kale

¼ beet, grated, or carrots

1 tablespoon finely chopped cranberries or blueberries

½ cup filtered water

1 cup cooked pinto beans

1 cup cooked buckwheat or quinoa

2 tablespoons peeled and chopped cucumber

DRESSING

MAKES APPROXIMATELY 3 SERVINGS

2 tablespoons organic tahini

½ teaspoon SuperYeastDust (page 145)

1 tablespoon filtered water

TOPPING

1 teaspoon chopped fresh basil

DIRECTIONS

In a skillet over medium heat, sauté kale, beets, and cranberries with water just until tender. Drain and cool to room temperature. Lightly mash beans in a bowl with a fork. Add in cooked buckwheat, cucumber, and cooled vegetables and mix to combine.

TO SERVE

Place proper portion for your dog in feeding bowl (see Feeding Chart on page 49). Place dressing ingredients in a small bowl and whisk with a fork. Add 1 teaspoon of the dressing to the feeding bowl. Sprinkle on basil and toss. Store in an airtight glass container or ziplock bag in the refrigerator for up to 3 days or freeze for up to 1 month.

TUSCAN BOWL

Spelt is an ancient grain that is high in fiber and protein. Although not gluten-free, it is higher in protein and minerals than wheat, and is easier to digest. It's a good substitute when used in moderation and will add variety and a different texture in your dog's diet.

MAKES 3 CUPS

1 cup cooked gluten-free spelt pasta
½ cup kale, stems removed
½ cup filtered water
1 cup cooked and mashed white beans
¼ cup chopped red bell pepper

TOPPING

1 teaspoon chopped fresh basil
¼ teaspoon olive oil
SuperYeastDust (page 145):
- ⅛ teaspoon for dogs up to 10 pounds
- ¼ teaspoon for dogs 20 to 40 pounds
- ½ teaspoon for dogs 50 to 80 pounds

DIRECTIONS

Cook pasta, drain, and chop into bite-size pieces. In skillet over medium heat, braise kale in water until tender. Turn off stove and add in mashed white beans and pasta. Add in chopped raw red bell pepper and mix in.

TO SERVE

Place proper portion for your dog in feeding bowl (see Feeding Chart on page 49). Top with basil, drizzle with olive oil, and sprinkle with SuperYeastDust. Store in an airtight glass container or ziplock bag in the refrigerator for up to 3 days or freeze for up to 1 month.

A MAN'S MEAL

This is a hearty meal full of nutrition. A great recipe to make extra batches of and freeze. Always remember to add in SuperBoosts, SuperDusts, or any supplements, fresh at each meal for maximum benefits.

MAKES 8 CUPS

1 cup dried lentils

1 cup quinoa

5½ cups filtered water

½ cup gluten-free oats

1 small sweet potato, peeled and chopped small

1 zucchini, chopped

1 cup finely chopped broccoli (including stems)

2 celery stalks, finely chopped

½ cup frozen peas

½ cup frozen cranberries

1 cup finely chopped mixed dark leafy greens

TOPPING

SuperBoost (page 144) and Super-YeastDust (page 145):

- ⅛ teaspoon of each boost/dust for dogs up to 10 pounds
- ¼ teaspoon of each boost/dust for dogs 20 to 40 pounds
- ½ teaspoon of each boost/dust for dogs 50 to 80 pounds

DIRECTIONS

Separately, rinse the lentils and quinoa. In a large pot over medium heat, add lentils and 4 cups of water and bring to a boil. Turn down heat and simmer with lid on for 15 minutes. Remove lid and add 1 more cup of water along with quinoa and oats. Bring back to a boil and then lower heat and simmer for 15 minutes. Taste for doneness. When finished cooking, let cool. In a separate pot, add the remaining ½ cup water and lightly cook sweet potato. Add in zucchini, broccoli, celery, frozen peas, cranberries, and leafy greens and steam until just barely tender. Mix vegetables together with the lentil-quinoa-oat mixture.

TO SERVE

Place proper portion for your dog in feeding bowl (see Feeding Chart on page 49), and mix in SuperBoost and SuperYeastDust. Store in an airtight glass container or ziplock bag in the refrigerator for up to 3 days or freeze for up to 1 month.

LUCKY ME

Brussels sprouts are loaded with vitamins A, B, C, and K, as well as minerals and a significant amount of antioxidants. Best served cooked and rotated into your dog's diet in moderation.

MAKES 3 CUPS

1 cup cooked mashed white beans

1 cup cooked quinoa, buckwheat, or amaranth

½ cup steamed and finely chopped Brussels sprouts

½ small sweet red pepper, finely chopped

1 to 2 teaspoons tahini

TOPPING

2 tablespoons chopped fresh basil

SuperYeastDust (page 145) :

- ⅛ teaspoon for dogs up to 10 pounds
- ¼ teaspoon for dogs 20 to 40 pounds
- ½ teaspoon for dogs 50 to 80 pounds

DIRECTIONS

In a large bowl, mix all the ingredients except toppings.

TO SERVE

Place proper portion for your dog in feeding bowl (see Feeding Chart on page 49), and add basil and SuperYeastDust toppings. Lightly mix and serve. Store in an airtight glass container or ziplock bag in the refrigerator for up to 3 days or freeze for up to 1 month.

REMY'S PICK

Mushrooms are one of the most nutritionally rich foods. Store-bought mushrooms, such as cremini, are safe for humans and dogs to eat. Never feed your dog wild mushrooms as they can be toxic to humans and dogs.

MAKES 4 CUPS

1 cup cooked lentils

1 cup cooked garbanzo beans

1 cup cooked quinoa, buckwheat, or amaranth

1 cup chopped broccoli

1 cup chopped spinach

1 medium zucchini, chopped

2 small cremini mushrooms chopped

TOPPING

1 tablespoon finely chopped sunflower sprouts or fresh basil

Pinch of dulse or kelp

¼ to 1 teaspoon flaxseed oil

SuperYeastDust (page 145):

- ⅛ teaspoon for dogs up to 10 pounds
- ¼ teaspoon for dogs 20 to 40 pounds
- ½ teaspoon for dogs 50 to 80 pounds

DIRECTIONS

In a large mixing bowl, combine cooked lentils, garbanzo beans, and quinoa. Clean and roughly chop broccoli, spinach, zucchini, and mushrooms. Lightly steam in a medium pot over medium heat until tender. Place all vegetables in a food processor and chop, leaving a little texture. Fold vegetables into the lentil-garbanzo-quinoa mixture and lightly stir.

TO SERVE

Place proper portion for your dog in feeding bowl (see Feeding Chart on page 49), and top with sunflower sprouts, a pinch of dulse, and flaxseed oil, and sprinkle with SuperYeastDust. Store in an airtight glass container or ziplock bag in the refrigerator for up to 3 days or freeze for up to 1 month.

MUFFINS

This is one healthy muffin! They are so good, we advise making an extra batch for yourself. We used a mini-muffin tin.

MAKES 12 MUFFINS

1 tablespoon flaxseed meal

3 tablespoons filtered water

1 cup cooked lentils

¾ cup gluten-free oatmeal

¾ cup quinoa flour

2 carrots, grated

2 zucchini, grated

2 teaspoons SuperHerbDust (page 145)

1 tablespoon organic coconut oil, plus a bit extra for greasing

TOPPING

Sprinkle of pumpkin seeds

1 handful of finely chopped spinach

TAHINI DRESSING

MAKES 1 SERVING

½ teaspoon tahini

¼ teaspoon SuperYeastDust (page 145)

2 teaspoons filtered water

DIRECTIONS

Preheat oven to 350°F. Mix flaxseed meal together with water to make a flax egg and let it sit for 5 to 7 minutes until thickened. Grease a mini muffin tin or small rame-kins with a bit of the coconut oil. Mix lentils, oatmeal, and quinoa flour together with the carrots, zucchini, SuperHerbDust, flax egg, and coconut oil. Form round balls to fit into muffin tins. Place a few pumpkin seeds on top of each muffin. Bake for 30 minutes. Remove from oven and let cool. Serve warm or at room temperature.

TO SERVE

Place a handful of chopped spinach in dog's serving bowl. Mix together the tahini dressing ingredients in a small bowl. Break up muffins into bite-size pieces and mix in dressing. Store in an airtight glass container or ziplock bag in the refrigerator for up to 3 days or freeze for up to 1 month.

TIP: Muffins can also be used as a snack.

SPANISH PAELLA

A colorful and flavorful, healthy meal for your dog (and you . . .). There are so many nutrients in all the various vegetables, it's like eating a multivitamin!

MAKES 4 CUPS

1 teaspoon organic coconut oil

½ sweet red pepper, chopped

1 carrot, chopped

6 cremini mushrooms, chopped

½ cup chopped asparagus

½ cup fresh or frozen peas

1 cup cooked mashed cannellini beans

1 cup cooked brown rice or quinoa

½ teaspoon SuperHerbDust (page 145)

TOPPING

SuperYeastDust (page 145):

- ⅛ teaspoon for dogs up to 10 pounds
- ¼ teaspoon for dogs 20 to 40 pounds
- ½ teaspoon for dogs 50 to 80 pounds

DIRECTIONS

In a skillet over medium heat, melt coconut oil and add red pepper, carrot, mushrooms, and asparagus. Cook until soft. Fold in peas, beans, rice, and SuperHerbDust to warm.

TO SERVE

Place proper portion for your dog in feeding bowl (see Feeding Chart on page 49). Sprinkle on SuperYeastDust. Store in an airtight glass container or ziplock bag in the refrigerator for up to 3 days or freeze for up to 1 month.

VEGETABLE KABOB AND CHICKPEA QUINOA

A dog's version of a kabob, minus the skewer. These are typical vegetables you will often see on a kabob. Served over quinoa and garbanzo beans, this meal is a complete protein.

MAKES 3 CUPS

1 zucchini, chopped

1 carrot, thinly cut on the diagonal

3 cremini or brown mushrooms, chopped

1 red pepper, finely chopped

¼ cup filtered water

½ teaspoon organic coconut oil

⅛ teaspoon turmeric

Pinch of SuperHerbDust (page 145)

1 cup cooked and lightly mashed garbanzo beans

1 cup cooked quinoa, buckwheat, or amaranth

TOPPING

Sprinkle of hemp hearts

Sprinkle of SuperYeastDust (page 145)

DIRECTIONS

Lightly steam vegetables in a medium pot over medium heat in a light broth of water, coconut oil, turmeric, and SuperHerbDust until tender. Mix in mashed garbanzo beans and fold in cooked quinoa.

TO SERVE

Place proper portion for your dog in feeding bowl (see Feeding Chart on page 49), and sprinkle with hemp hearts and SuperYeastDust. Lightly mix together. Store in an airtight glass container or ziplock bag in the refrigerator for up to 3 days or freeze for up to 1 month.

TIP: This can also be cooked on a grill or BBQ. In that case, add vegetables to a skewer, lightly brush with coconut oil, and sprinkle with SuperHerbDust. Cook until tender. When feeding to your dog, cool to room temperature, and always remove skewer. Sprinkle with hemp hearts and SuperYeastDust and serve over chickpea quinoa.

CHOPPED QUINOA SALAD

Dogs love salad too, especially when it's tossed in a calcium-boosting tahini dressing. Chop vegetables fine for easy digestion.

MAKES 3 CUPS

1 cup cooked pinto beans

1 cup cooked quinoa

½ cup finely chopped romaine lettuce

½ carrot, gated

¼ small cucumber, finely chopped

¼ red bell pepper, finely chopped

¼ cup finely chopped celery

1 tablespoon pureed or finely chopped fresh or frozen cranberries

DRESSING

MAKES 1 SERVING

2 tablespoons filtered water

½ teaspoon tahini

Pinch of SuperHerbDust (page 145)

Pinch of SuperYeast Dust (page 145)

DIRECTIONS

Place all salad ingredients in a mixing bowl and toss.

TO SERVE

Place proper portion for your dog in feeding bowl (see Feeding Chart on page 49). Mix together all dressing ingredients and lightly toss once more. Store in an airtight glass container or ziplock bag in the refrigerator for up to 3 days.

BLACK BEAN SALAD WITH RICE BOWL

Black beans provide a healthy source of calories and plant protein. Chopped red pepper adds a little crunch as well as vitamin A, which helps support healthy vision, vitamin C, which supports immunity, and vitamin E, which benefits your dog's skin and coat.

MAKES 3 CUPS

1 cup cooked black beans

1 cup cooked brown rice or quinoa

1 carrot, grated

½ zucchini, grated or spiralized and chopped

½ red pepper, finely diced

½ cup finely chopped cabbage, lettuce, or spinach

DRESSING

MAKES 1 SERVING

½ teaspoon flaxseed oil

Pinch of SuperHerbDust (page 145)

Pinch of SuperYeastDust (page 145)

DIRECTIONS

In a large bowl, mix together beans, rice, carrot, zucchini, red pepper, and cabbage.

TO SERVE

Place proper portion for your dog in feeding bowl (see Feeding Chart on page 49). Mix together ingredients for dressing and drizzle over bowl. Store in an airtight glass container or ziplock bag in the refrigerator for up to 3 days or freeze for up to 1 month.

BUFFET SALAD BAR BOWL

Quinoa, buckwheat, and amaranth are called "pseudograins." They resemble grains, but are actually seeds and do not contain gluten. Quinoa by itself is considered a complete protein, as it has all the essential amino acids.

MAKES 1 SERVING

Choose a protein: lentils or beans

Choose a seed: quinoa, buckwheat, or amaranth

Choose a green: spinach or romaine, chopped

Choose a vegetable: carrots or cooked green beans, chopped

Choose an oil: flaxseed or hemp

Choose a sprinkle of SuperHerbDust (page 145) or SuperYeastDust (page 145)

DIRECTIONS

Place selection from each category in a mixing bowl, toss together, and serve in your dog's favorite bowl. For example, when feeding a 10-pound dog: use 4 tablespoons of lentils, 4 tablespoons of quinoa, 1 tablespoon spinach, 1 tablespoon carrots, ¼ teaspoon flaxseed oil, and a sprinkle of SuperYeastDust.

MORE PLEASE BOWL

A microplane is a great tool, as it quickly grates carrots, beets, or zucchini as a topper on any dish.

MAKES 3 CUPS OF LENTIL BASE

2 cups cooked lentils

1 cup cooked quinoa, buckwheat or amaranth

TOPPING

2 tablespoons finely chopped spinach

1 tablespoon microplaned carrot or other vegetable

1 tablespoon finely chopped sunflower sprouts

⅛ teaspoon flaxseed oil

⅛ teaspoon SuperBoost (page 144)

⅛ teaspoon SuperYeastDust (page 145)

DIRECTIONS

In a food processor, lightly puree lentils. Place in a bowl and mix in quinoa.

TO SERVE

Place proper portion of lentil-quinoa mixture for your dog in feeding bowl (see Feeding Chart on page 49), and add remaining ingredients. Store in an airtight glass container or ziplock bag in the refrigerator for up to 3 days or freeze for up to 1 month.

COMFORT BOWL

Here is an easy way to cook butternut squash, which is high in beta-carotene, and may assist in preventing cancer as well as providing healthy benefits for your dog's heart.

MAKES 5 CUPS

1 butternut or acorn squash

¼ cup water

1 zucchini, diced in cubes

1 carrot, diced in cubes

½ beet, diced in cubes

1 cup chopped kale, stems removed

1 cup cooked kidney beans

1 cup cooked quinoa, buckwheat, or amaranth

DRESSING

MAKES 1 SERVING

1 teaspoon tahini

⅛ teaspoon turmeric

⅛ teaspoon SuperYeastDust (page 145)

2 tablespoons filtered water

DIRECTIONS

Preheat oven to 375°F. Cut squash in half, leaving seeds in while cooking. Place cut side up on a cookie sheet and bake for 25 minutes. Combine ¼ cup water, zucchini, carrot, beet, and kale in a baking dish. After squash has cooked for 25 minutes, place casserole dish of vegetables in oven and cook both squash and vegetables for an additional 25 minutes. Remove vegetables from the oven and test the squash for tenderness. If soft, remove from oven and cool. Once cool, remove seeds and discard. Scoop out squash and mix together with vegetables, kidney beans, and quinoa.

TO SERVE

Place proper portion for your dog in feeding bowl (see Feeding Chart on page 49). Stir together all dressing ingredients and drizzle on the veggies. Store in an airtight glass container or ziplock bag in the refrigerator for up to 3 days or freeze for up to 1 month.

HAPPY DOG BOWL

Sweet potatoes are full of fiber and are great for your dog's digestive health. They are loaded with beta-carotene, which is important for your dog's vision. Cutting sweet potato into small cubes allows the potato to cook faster and easily mixes with other ingredients.

MAKES 5 CUPS

1 teaspoon chia seeds

2 tablespoons filtered water

1 cup cooked lentils

1 cup cooked chickpeas

1 cup cooked quinoa, buckwheat, or amaranth

1 cup cooked and peeled sweet potato, diced in cubes

¼ cup carrot, diced

¼ cup red pepper, diced

¼ cup cranberries, diced

TOPPING

¼ cup finely chopped romaine lettuce

Sprinkle of SuperBoost (page 144)

Sprinkle of SuperYeastDust (page 145)

DIRECTIONS

Cover chia seeds with water and set aside to gel for 3 to 5 minutes. Combine cooked lentils, chickpeas, quinoa, and sweet potato. Add in carrot, red pepper, and cranberries. Mix in chia gel.

TO SERVE

Place proper portion for your dog in feeding bowl (see Feeding Chart on page 49), and top with lettuce and a sprinkle of SuperBoost and SuperYeastDust. Stir gently to combine all ingredients and serve. Store in an airtight glass container or ziplock bag in the refrigerator for up to 3 days or freeze for up to 1 month.

STIR-FRY BOWL

No need to order take-out when you can make this quick meal for you and the pooch. Broccoli is full of nutrients and rich in antioxidants that can help fight inflammation, cancer, and allergies. As with any vegetable, it's important to rotate a variety of vegetables in your dog's diet. (If you need a little more season-ing for yourself, drizzle a little bit of organic coconut aminos on your portion.) Adding kombu seaweed to the cooking beans not only enhances the flavor, it also reduces the gas-producing properties of the beans. Place a kombu strip in the pot of beans before boiling and remove once the beans have cooked.

MAKES 3 CUPS

½ cup finely chopped broccoli

2 carrots, finely chopped

3 cremini mushrooms, finely chopped

¼ cup chopped bean sprouts

1 cup cooked mung beans (cooked with piece of kombu; see headnote)

1 cup cooked brown rice or quinoa

TOPPING

Pinch of chopped fresh basil or mint leaves

DRESSING

MAKES 3 TO 4 SERVINGS

1 teaspoon unsalted sunflower seed or peanut butter

2 tablespoons filtered water

¼ teaspoon SuperYeastDust (page 145)

DIRECTIONS

In a medium pan over medium heat, lightly sauté broccoli, carrots, and mushrooms in ⅓ cup water until tender. In a bowl, combine cooked vegetables, bean sprouts, mung beans, and rice. Toss ingredients to combine.

TO SERVE

Place proper portion for your dog in feeding bowl (see Feeding Chart on page 49). Top with fresh basil. To make the dressing, stir all ingredients together in a small bowl until smooth. Drizzle the dressing over the meal, stir in, and serve. Store in an airtight glass container or ziplock bag in the refrigerator for up to 3 days.

ASH SOUP

This meal is inspired by Ash Reshteh, a thick Persian soup, which is often served in winter and for the Persian New Year. For your dog, serve cold or slightly warmed, just above room temperature.

MAKES 4 CUPS

2 tablespoons filtered water
1 cup chopped spinach or kale
⅛ teaspoon turmeric
Pinch of SuperHerbDust (page 145)
1 cup cooked lentils
½ cup cooked garbanzo beans
½ cup cooked kidney beans
1 cup cooked quinoa or barley

¼ teaspoon chopped parsley or sunflower sprouts

DRESSING

MAKES 1 SERVING

½ teaspoon tahini
1 to 2 tablespoons filtered water
⅛ teaspoon SuperYeastDust (page 145)

DIRECTIONS

Place water into a pan over medium heat and lightly sauté spinach with turmeric and SuperHerbDust. In a mixing bowl, mix lentils, beans, and quinoa, then add spinach and chopped parsley. Stir gently to combine.

TO SERVE

Place proper portion for your dog in feeding bowl (see Feeding Chart on page 49). To make the dressing, stir all ingredients together and lightly mix in dressing. Store in an airtight glass container in the refrigerator for up to 3 days or freeze for up to 1 month.

MEALTIME ADDITIONS

———o———

THE FOLLOWING RECIPES CAN BE MIXED INTO ANY MEAL TO ADD NUTRIENTS and variety. Another easy trick is to grate in carrots, zucchini, or other fresh vegetables as a topping.

BROCCOLI SOUP

This soup can be served cold or slightly warmed. It can be eaten as a snack or poured over rice and beans for main meal bowls.

MAKES 2 CUPS

2 cups roughly chopped broccoli
1 cup filtered water
1 tablespoon tahini
¼ teaspoon kelp or dulse

TOPPING

Sprinkle of SuperBoost (page 144)
Sprinkle of SuperYeastDust (page 145)

DIRECTIONS

In a large pot over medium heat, lightly steam chopped broccoli until just tender. Place broccoli and cooking water in blender. Add tahini and kelp, and puree to soup texture, adding more water as needed.

TO SERVE

Depending on the size of your dog, feed 1 to 3 tablespoons as a snack, sprinkled with SuperBoost and SuperYeastDust, or add to any main meal. Store in an airtight glass container or ziplock bag in the refrigerator for up to 3 days or freeze for up to 1 month.

CALCIUM BROTH

Calcium is essential in a dog's diet, as it's been proven to relieve joint pain, support and repair cartilage, reduce inflammation, and improve flexibility. If your dog needs more calcium in their diet, this recipe is a great addition. Our plant-based broth contains vegetables that are high in calcium. Broth can be slightly warmed and poured over food to moisten your dog's meal. This broth can be frozen in ice cube trays and stored in ziplock bags.

MAKES 10 CUPS

10 cups filtered water
1 cup roughly chopped collard greens
1 cup roughly chopped bok choy
1 cup roughly chopped kale

1 cup roughly chopped broccoli
1 teaspoon kelp
Generous pinch of SuperHerbDust
  (page 145)

DIRECTIONS

Place all ingredients in a large pot and cook on low heat. Turn off heat when vegetables start to soften, about 15 minutes. Let cool and place 2 cups of cooking water and all vegetables in a blender, reserving the rest of the cooking water. Blend until smooth. Pour vegetable puree back into the cooking water and stir.

TO SERVE

Depending on the size of your dog, serve 1 to 3 tablespoons as a snack or add to any main meal. Store in an airtight glass container or ziplock bag in the refrigerator for up to 3 days or freeze for up to 3 months.

CAULIFLOWER RICE

It's always a good idea to introduce new vegetables into your dog's diet. Cauliflower, a cruciferous vegetable that can block cancer cells from spreading and is full of vitamins and fiber, is a great one to try if your dog has never had it before. Cauliflower rice is not a replacement for rice or grains, but can add the same texture. Sprinkle over or mix into any meal.

MAKES 1½ CUPS

½ small cauliflower
Choice of turmeric, SuperHerbDust
    (page 145), fresh ginger, cilantro,
    or basil

DIRECTIONS

There are three methods to turn the cauliflower into rice-size pieces. One is with a box grater and the others are with a food processor grater attachment or by simply pulse-chopping. Rinse off cauliflower, remove stem and leaves, and pat dry. Break into large buds and process into rice. If using a food processor, use the grater attachment or pulse-chop in two batches so as not to pulverize the pieces too small. Do not over-chop or else the cauliflower will have the consistency of mashed potatoes (see below for that process). For the box grater method, grate desired amount. Cauliflower Rice can be cooked in a pan with 1 to 2 tablespoons of filtered water. Cook for 5 minutes, then remove from heat, mix in seasoning of choice, place lid on, and steam for 5 minutes. Store in an airtight glass container or ziplock bag in the refrigerator for up to 2 days or freeze for up to 1 month.

MASHED CAULIFLOWER

MAKES 1 CUP

Follow same directions as above, except pulse-chop in food processor until the consistency of mash potatoes. Heat and add seasoning of choice.

MUSHROOM GRAVY

Mushroom Gravy is a little extra treat to moisten your pup's food.

1 tablespoon coconut oil

1 cup very finely chopped white button mushrooms

1 tablespoon coconut flour

1 cup Calcium Broth (page 113)

DIRECTIONS

In a skillet, heat oil over medium heat and sauté mushrooms until tender. Stir in coconut flour and cook for 1 minute. Add broth and reduce heat. Simmer until thickened, then remove from heat.

TO SERVE

Gravy can be added to any meal bowl. Feed in moderation once or twice a week. Use 1 teaspoon for small dogs and 2 teaspoons for larger dogs. Store in an airtight glass container in the refrigerator for up to 3 days or freeze for up to 1 month.

——⸗ SARAH AND HER MANY DOGS ⸒——

*Sarah Schell is the owner of LoVegano, a vegan supermarket in
Palma de Mallorca, Spain*

For many years now, my dogs have been fed a 100 percent vegetable diet. In most cases, they are much healthier than those that are fed on standard kibble or meat-based diets. Plant-based food can offer a varied diet with all the properties and nutrition for different breeds and sizes, plus a range of flavors that satisfies our furry ones. Looking at the question of health, any veterinarian could confirm many terrifying cases of animals getting sick from diabetes or dying from cancer. It seems that we have "given" our pets the same diseases that our society has and this is evidently for lack of information regarding a healthy diet.

In my case, with almost five years of experience working with eight vegan dogs, I want to advise this type of feeding for all dogs.

ALL ANIMALS WISH TO LIVE.

KIMCHI FOR DOGS

It's crucial for dogs to have good gut bacteria. Probiotics also support the brain, digestion, immune system, and assimilation of nutrients. Fermented foods are great for dogs as well as humans. Our doggie Kimchi does not contain salt. We use celery juice, kelp, and dulse to help release the water in the vegetables during fermentation.

MAKES 3 CUPS

½ head Napa, Savoy, or regular white
    cabbage
1 carrot, grated
1 small apple, grated
½ small beet, grated

½ teaspoon dulse
½ teaspoon kelp
¼ teaspoon SuperHerbDust (page 145)
½ cup celery juice
Filtered water

DIRECTIONS

Wash and cut the cabbage in half lengthwise, reserving one cabbage leaf. Shred cabbage in a food processor or finely chop. In a large mixing bowl, add shredded cabbage, carrot, apple, and beet. Add in dulse, kelp, and SuperHerbDust. Pour celery juice over ingredients and stir gently to combine. Gently fill a mason jar with the mixture, pushing down to release any liquid. If there is not enough to cover, add a teaspoon or two of water. Place the reserved cabbage leaf on top of the mixture and cover jar with a loose-fitting lid. Let it sit in a cool area in the kitchen for 7 days. Check often to be sure the vegetables are covered with celery juice. This will help the fermentation process. The flavor will get stronger the longer it ferments. After 7 days of fermentation, put on tight-fitting lid and store in the refrigerator. Kimchi lasts a few months refrigerated, but it does get stronger.

TO SERVE

Kimchi can be added to any meal bowl. Feed in moderation once or twice a week. Use ½ teaspoon for small dogs and 1 teaspoon for larger dogs.

TREATS AND SNACKS

———o———

MOST OF THE DOG CHEWS ON THE SHELVES HAVE PRESERVATIVES OR CHEMICAL byproducts, and many have been recalled because dogs were getting sick from consuming them. Commercial dog treats are processed and lack nutrients. We have created some easy snacks and chew recipes to make in your own kitchen. They will delight and keep your pal healthy.

SWEET POTATO FRIES AND CHEWS

Sweet potatoes come in a variety of colors. You can find white, yellow, rust, and purple. The rust color skins have an orange interior while the white and yellow skins have a pale interior. The rust skin with orange color inside is the highest in beta-carotene. This is the sweet potato we prefer, as the texture is harder and when dried, it makes a great dog chew. Whichever you can find at your market will provide your dog with nutritional value. Sweet potatoes are high in vitamin A, B5, B6, thiamin, niacin, riboflavin, and, due to their orange color, carotenoids and beta-carotene. They also contain potassium, magnesium, and vitamin C, which helps to support a healthy immune system. Sweet potatoes are also a good source of dietary fiber and can help in maintaining a healthy digestive tract and regulate digestion.

2 large sweet potatoes, scrubbed
    clean
Sprinkle of SuperHerbDust (page 145)

DIRECTIONS

There are two methods for drying sweet potatoes. One is in a dehydrator and the other is in an oven. If using an oven, preheat oven to lowest temperature. Line a baking sheet with parchment paper.

Cut off the pointy ends of the potato. Cut down the middle lengthwise. Continue to cut lengthwise slices approximately ⅓- to ½-inch thick. They will shrink, so choose the larger size for larger dogs. Place slices on the prepared baking sheet and sprinkle with SuperHerbDust. Bake 1 to 2 hours, checking for doneness. The texture should not be too soft or too brittle. When done, remove the chews from the oven and let them cool and dry.

If using a dehydrator, spread sliced sweet potato on mesh dehydrator sheet and dehydrate 6 to 8 hours or until thoroughly dry at 115°F.

Store in a glass container with an airtight lid. These treats will last 2 weeks. No refrigeration necessary if they are brittle and completely dry. For a softer treat, bake or dry for a shorter period of time and refrigerate.

CANINE CRACKERS

This recipe can be made using your morning juice pulp, including spinach, romaine, kale, carrots, cucumber, and apple (without seeds or stem). If juicing other vegetables, check to see what might be toxic for dogs (page 45). Juice pulp can be frozen in an airtight glass container or plastic freezer bag until you collect what you need to make the crackers. You can also cut the recipe in half if you don't have enough pulp to make a full recipe.

MAKES 4 CUPS

6 to 8 cups finely chopped assorted vegetables (see headnote)

1 cup sunflower seeds, soaked for 2 to 3 hours

1 cup pumpkin seeds, soaked for 2 to 3 hours

1 teaspoon SuperHerbDust (page 145)

½ cup pureed or finely chopped fresh or frozen cranberries (optional)

1 cup flaxseed meal, soaked in 2 cups filtered water for ½ hour

DIRECTIONS

Place all ingredients, except soaked flaxseed meal, into a food processor and chop until combined. Place mixture into a bowl, add soaked flaxseed meal, and mix in well with a spatula. There are two methods for drying crackers. One is in a dehydrator and the other is in an oven. If using a dehydrator, spread mixture into a ¼-inch-thick layer onto a non-stick sheet. Score into 2- to 3-inch squares. This will make it easier to break apart evenly when dehydrated. Set heat at 145°F for 1 hour, reduce heat to 115°F, and dehydrate for approximately 8 hours until dry enough to flip over. Place a tray with mesh screen on top of cracker tray. Flip over so crackers are now on the mesh screen and peel off the non-stick sheet. If it is still wet in the center, use a spatula to help lift it off the sheet. Continue to dehydrate until completely dry.

If using an oven, set temperature at the lowest setting, line a baking sheet with parchment paper or a silpat mat, and spread crackers in a ¼-inch-thin layer onto the prepared sheet. Cook for 30 minutes and check for crispness and bake longer if needed. Check often so as not to burn the crackers.

For both methods, let cool and store in airtight glass container.

DESSERTS

———o———

AN OCCASIONAL HEALTHY DESSERT IS OKAY TO GIVE TO YOUR POOCH. PROVIDE them one of the following treats and you might see a smile on their face.

BANANA ICE CREAM

Some dogs go bananas for bananas and most every dog loves ice cream! This recipe is super easy to make, plus bananas are a potassium-rich, high-in-fiber fruit. They are a very good source of magnesium, which supports bone growth and helps the body produce protein and absorb vitamins. Feed in moderation because treats like bananas contain natural sugar.

MAKES 4 TO 5 SERVINGS

1 banana
Filtered water
Peanut butter or tahini (optional)

DIRECTIONS

Peel and break the banana into 3 to 4 pieces, seal it in a ziplock freezer bag, and place in the freezer. Freeze overnight. When ready to serve, place into food processor with a little water. Pulse-chop, adding water a teaspoon at a time until the desired smooth mixture is achieved. Stop once and scrape down with a spatula. A juicer with a homogenizing attachment can be used to make soft-serve ice cream. Mix in a little soft peanut butter or tahini for an extra treat. This should be served as a small treat, according to your dog's weight. For a 10-pound dog, for example, serve 2 tablespoons.

COOKIES COOKIES COOKIES

These cookies are SO easy to make you will always want to have them on hand for a treat. Try not to eat them all and leave some for your pal.

MAKES APPROXIMATELY 50 COOKIES

2 cups gluten-free oats

2 large ripe bananas

¼ cup pumpkin seeds

¼ cup unsweetened coconut flakes

2 teaspoons organic coconut oil

¼ cup chopped cranberries (optional)

DIRECTIONS

Preheat oven to 350°F. Line a baking sheet with parchment paper. Place 1½ cups oats in a food processor and add bananas, half of the pumpkin seeds, and half of the coconut flakes. Chop until combined. Place into a bowl with remaining oats, pumpkin seeds, coconut flakes, and coconut oil, and blend in with a fork until well combined. To make small cookies, use 1 teaspoon full of mixture and drop onto the prepared sheet. Place baking sheet on middle rack of oven and bake for 30 minutes. Test for doneness and, if you want the cookies crisper, leave in another 5 minutes.

BIRTHDAY CAKE

Happy Birthday! Celebrate your BFF's birthday and invite their friends over for a party. Human friends can enjoy a slice of this cake as well. Coconut cream can be purchased in most stores. Look for unsweetened organic.

SERVES 4 TO 6

2 cups filtered water

1 cup gluten-free oats

1 large ripe banana

1 cup shredded beets, for garnish

½ to ¾ cup unsweetened coconut cream, for frosting

DIRECTIONS

Use a 4-inch springform pan or 3-inch glass container. Rub pan with coconut oil.

Place water and oats in a pan over medium heat and cook until soft, stirring occasionally, for approximately 5 minutes. Turn off the heat, cover pan, and let steam for 4 minutes. In a bowl, mash banana with a fork until smooth. Mix well into oatmeal. Scoop oatmeal-banana mixture into a greased pan, press down, and smooth out. Cover with plastic wrap and refrigerate for 4 to 6 hours. Grate beets and place in a bowl. Cover and let sit to release liquid. Use an electric beater or wire whisk to whip coconut into a whipped cream. When cake has set, remove from pan and set on a plate. It should be jelled and solid. Frost the cake with the coconut whipped cream. Drain beets and pat dry. Press around the sides of the cake. Time for the birthday party! Otherwise, you can store it in an airtight glass container and refrigerate for up to 3 days.

STRAWBERRY HEARTS

Express your love with these beautiful jeweled strawberry hearts. This treat contains an abundance of vitamin C. Use to infuse water or blend in a smoothie.

MAKES 1 DOZEN

2 cups whole strawberries
2 teaspoons melted organic coconut oil

DIRECTIONS

Place ingredients in blender and blend until smooth. Pour into silicone mold and freeze. Once frozen, remove from mold and store in ziplock freezer bag in the freezer for up to 2 months.

FRUIT ICE CUBE TREATS

Another easy and healthy dessert to make for your pup.

MAKES 1 DOZEN

1 ripe banana
1–3 teaspoons of filtered water
Berries of choice

DIRECTIONS

Mash a ripe banana in a mixing bowl until smooth. Add 1-3 teaspoons of filtered water as needed. Spoon mixture into ice-cube trays and press a berry in each section. Blueberry, strawberry, or blackberry work well. Freeze until solid and serve as a treat. Once frozen, remove from ice-cube trays and store in ziplock freezer bag in the freezer for up to 2 months.

DOGGY JUICE AND HYDRATION

———·o·———

IF YOU ARE JUICING FOR YOURSELF AND EVER WONDERED IF JUICING WAS GOOD for your dog, the answer is yes, but only if you are juicing ingredients not toxic for dogs (see page 45 for a list of foods toxic to dogs). Water down the juice you made for yourself with equal parts filtered water. This makes it easy on your dog's digestion. Two to 4 tablespoons of watered-down juice for a 10-pound dog is sufficient. This can be served as a healthy treat, or you can pour it into your dog's meal.

DOGGIE SMOOTHIE

Hemp seeds provide protein, bananas provide potassium, and berries are high in antioxidants, which makes this smoothie a powerhouse of nutrients.

MAKES 3 TO 4 SERVINGS

¾ cup filtered water

½ banana

¼ cup berries of choice

1 teaspoon hemp seeds

DIRECTIONS

Place all ingredients in a blender and blend until smooth.

INFUSED VITAMIN WATERS

Keep yourself and your dog hydrated. If you would like your dog to drink more water, this is a good way to get them to do so. Flavored water is tastier than plain water. The water will also have vitamin content so it's a win-win for your darling tail-wagger.

CUCUMBER WATER

Place several slices of peeled cucumber into a quart-size jar of filtered water. Store in refrigerator overnight. Remove cucumbers in the morning and discard or eat as a treat.

BLUEBERRY WATER

Place several blueberries into a quart-size jar of filtered water. Store in refrigerator overnight. Remove blueberries in the morning and discard or eat as a treat.

CELERY WATER

Cut 1 stalk of celery in half and place into a quart-size jar of filtered water. Store in refrigerator overnight. Remove celery in the morning and discard or eat as a treat.

BASIL WATER

Place 3 to 4 basil leaves into a quart-size jar of filtered water. Store in refrigerator overnight. Remove leaves in the morning and discard.

CARROT WATER

Pour a little carrot juice in your dog's water. This high-nutrient vitamin water will be a very healthy addition to your dog's diet.

DUSTS AND BOOSTS

———o———

JUST AS FOR HUMANS, FRESH ORGANIC FOOD IS ALWAYS BEST, BUT EVEN SO, sometimes we need supplements to complete our nutritional needs. We present four different superfoods for you to make in your own kitchen. The following recipes for SuperBoost and Dusts are important components of your pup's health. They are easy to assemble and can be stored in a glass jar with a tight-fitting lid. Store them in the refrigerator as suggested or a dark dry place in your cupboard. Amounts to be used will be listed in the recipes. You can purchase the ingredients to make SuperBoost and SuperDusts online or at your health food store. Always buy organic and see page 43 for a recommended source when purchasing spirulina. Also, check our A–Z Glossary Unleashed on page 153 for the nutritional value of each item. Use SuperBoost and SuperDusts to enhance your dog's protein and nutrient intake.

SuperBoost

This SuperBoost is anti-inflammatory, rich in protein, and high in antioxidants.

MAKES APPROXIMATELY 1 CUP

4 tablespoons hemp hearts   4 tablespoons pumpkin seeds
4 tablespoons sunflower seeds   1 tablespoon spirulina

DIRECTIONS

Place everything but the spirulina into a blender, coffee grinder, or food processor. Grind gently to a dust-like consistency. Add in spirulina and blend all ingredients together. Store in an airtight glass jar in the refrigerator and mark SuperBoost on the container along with the date. You can keep in the fridge for 3 months. Shake each time before using, as ingredients settle.

NOTE: You can alternate between SuperBoost and SuperSeedDust in recipes.

SuperSeedDust

SuperSeedDust contains protein, omega-3 fatty acids, potassium, magnesium, selenium, calcium, iron, zinc, and antioxidants. Just as for humans, fresh organic food is always best.

MAKES 1 CUP

4 tablespoons hemp hearts   4 tablespoons chia seeds
4 tablespoons sunflower seeds   4 tablespoons flax seeds
4 tablespoons pumpkin seeds   1 brazil nut

DIRECTIONS

Place all ingredients into a blender, coffee grinder, or food processor. Do not over-process—just break down the nut and seeds. Store in a glass container with an airtight lid in the refrigerator and mark SuperSeedDust on the container along with the date. You can keep in the fridge for 3 months. Shake each time before using, as ingredients settle.

SuperHerbDust

Herbs have healing medicinal properties, including boosting the immune system and improving digestion. Some herbs even repel insects. This mixture is called for in many of our recipes, but can be used in any savory meal to lift the flavors and strengthen your dog's body. Always use high quality organic herbs and omit rosemary if your dog suffers from seizures or is pregnant.

MAKES ¾ CUP

2 tablespoons dried oregano

2 tablespoons dried thyme

2 tablespoons dried basil

1 teaspoon dried rosemary

1 teaspoon dried parsley

1 tablespoon dried dulse or kelp

DIRECTIONS

Mix ingredients together. Store in a glass container with an airtight lid in a dark, dry place in your cupboard for up to 3 months. Shake each time before using, as ingredients settle.

TIP: Add in ground fennel seeds as needed to help calm your dog's digestive tract and relieve gas.

SuperYeastDust

Our SuperYeastDust contains vitamin B12 and other B vitamins. It's good for heart and brain health as well as inflammation. It is always best to use organic ingredients.

MAKES 1½ CUPS

1 cup nutritional yeast

¼ cup barley grass powder

1 tablespoon sunflower lecithin

½ teaspoon dried thyme

DIRECTIONS

Mix ingredients together. Store in a glass container with an airtight lid in a dark, dry place in your cupboard for up to 3 months. Shake each time before using, as ingredients settle.

SUPERKALEDUST

This can be sprinkled on any main meal recipe as a topping. It also mixes well with SuperYeastDust.

1 bunch of kale

DIRECTIONS

Preheat oven to lowest temperature or use a dehydrator. Wash, dry, and de-stem kale. Break into large pieces. Place kale in a single layer on an ungreased baking sheet (more than one baking sheet may be needed) and bake until dry and crunchy, approximately 10 to 15 minutes.

Alternatively, place on mesh sheet of dehydrator and set temperature to 115°F. Dehydrate until crisp, approximately 4 to 6 hours. When dry, place in food processor and pulverize into a powder. Store in a glass container with an airtight lid in a dark, dry place in your cupboard for up to 3 months.

Afterword

———o———

Thank you for your compassion for all living things and our environment.

With much love,
Mimi and Lisa

Acknowledgments

———o———

We want to thank our amazing family, Jonas, Mia, Dan, Gigi, Luke, Audrey, Karly, Rocky, and Gunner. They have encouraged us throughout this book. Special thanks to Mackenzie Kirk for beautiful early edits and writing; to Hannah Kirk, our dog photographer, who loves dogs and they love her: We love all your hundreds of shots and it was a challenge to choose which ones would go into the book. Thanks to the ever present and always-ready-to-lend-a-hand Mike Mendell, for always taking beautiful food photos and for your constant patience and support. Thank you to Kari Stuart, our literary agent at ICM—we are lucky to have your support and encouragement. Ann Treistman, editorial director, and Aurora Bell, associate editor, at The Countryman Press. A big thank you to Susie Lopez, who did such a beautiful job organizing our first doggy casting call. Special thanks to Molly and Elan for taking time out of your busy schedules and for your directorial skills with your two adorable dogs. Deep thanks to all the dogs and doggy parents who came out for our photo shoots and recipe tests.

Mimi: It was my co-writer, Lisa, who piqued my interest in dogs and dog food. I thank you so much for this gift. I have loved writing with you and eating dog food with you. My longtime friends Julie Kavner and Robin Leech (RIP) have always been a part of my life and my book collaborations. On my side for this journey, to my friends who listened, made me laugh, and supported me: Cat, Miriam, Sue, Sarah, Corinna, and all my vegan pet parents, veterinarians, and advocates who helped along the way.

ACKNOWLEDGMENTS

Lisa: Heartfelt thanks to the ones I love for all their support on this project. Mom, thanks for being the best teacher about life and for the gift of writing this book with you. Huge shoutout to Ruthanne (for so many things) and Much Love Animal Rescue for saving Bianca's life, being on the front-lines, and doing all they can to rescue animals every day. Thanks to Stacy, for saving dogs and always shinning light; Denise, for your cheerleading and baton twirling; the lovely Gigi and Diego, Joe, Liezel, Flora, Glory, and the garden. And love to Robert, for teaching me how to cook dog food and people food, which is really just the same.

A–Z Glossary Unleashed

———°———

Learn which foods are good for dogs and which foods are toxic and should be avoided. As you gain knowledge of the nutritional value in the foods you feed your pup, you will also build the confidence you need in your dog's completely balanced, plant-based diet.

Feeding your dog a clean, fresh whole-food diet puts your dog ahead of the game. Moderation and variety are key.

Amaranth: Amaranth is known as one of the super-grains, and is actually a seed. It's gluten-free and high in fiber and protein. It is also rich in calcium, iron, phosphorus, carotenoids, manganese, and potassium, which mixes well with other grains and helps to maintain steady blood sugar levels.

Apple Cider Vinegar: Apple cider vinegar is fermented, so make sure you buy it raw, organic, and unpasteurized. Fermented foods are great for digestion. The sedimentation floating on the bottom of the bottle is known as the Mother, which is what puts the good bacteria and enzymes in the vinegar. Apple cider vinegar helps with gas and bloating, and regulates digestion.

Apples: Not only are they a crunchy treat, apples are extremely rich in important antioxidants, flavonoids, and dietary fiber. An article published on *Medical News Today* in 2017 stated that the phytonutrients and antioxidants in apples may help reduce the risk of developing cancer, heart disease, and diabetes. They also can aid in detoxifying and removing heavy metals such as lead and mercury. Apples help to clean residue off dogs' teeth and freshen their breath. They contain vitamins A, C, and

K, phosphorus, iron flavonoids, and calcium. Avoid feeding your dog the seeds, core, and stem from the apple, as they contain cyanide and are toxic. Dehydrated apples have no water, so make sure you only feed your pup very small bits or soak them in water to re-hydrate beforehand. There are many different ways to feed apple to dogs: You can serve it as a frozen slice or you can wedge it into a Kong, which is a toy you stuff with food to keep your dog entertained. As they play with their toy for a while, the food works its way out. You can also freeze unsweetened applesauce and make apple pops or serve it grated over a breakfast bowl.

Asparagus: Asparagus contains folate, copper, selenium, and vitamins B1, B2, B3, B6, A, C, E, and K. It is a good source of fiber, phosphorus, manganese, potassium, choline, zinc, iron, and protein. Asparagus has a high amount of amino acids and can help prevent urinary infections. Undercook to maintain the antioxidant properties. Pulse-chop in a food processor before serving or chop finely with a knife.

Bananas: Bananas contain vitamins B, C, potassium, and magnesium. Bananas are high in natural digestible sugar and are a good source of manganese, vitamin B6, C, fiber, biotin, and copper. Bananas are best used as a treat.

Barley: Although not as popular as other whole grains, barley has some good health benefits, including protein. This ancient grain is high in antioxidants, fiber, selenium, copper, magnesium, phosphorus, chromium, niacin, and trace minerals. It contains vitamins B1 and B3. The best way to get the most nutrients from barley is to soak and sprout the hulled grain. This helps unleash the nutrients so the body can absorb and use the vitamins found in the grain.

Barley Grass Powder: The chlorophyll in barley grass can help improve your dog's digestion and breath. It is rich in A, B, and C vitamins and essential trace minerals, which can help promote healthy skin and coat.

Basil: Basil can help relieve gas and soothe an upset stomach. It may be useful in treating arthritis and inflammatory bowel diseases, since it reduces swelling. Basil has antioxidant and antiviral properties. It also repels mosquitoes, fleas, and other insects.

Beans: Cannellini, pinto, black, white, kidney, garbanzo, and mung are popular beans that contain a multitude of healthy properties. Beans are a powerhouse of nutrients packed with protein, antioxidants, fiber, folate, potassium, magnesium, copper, and zinc. In a vegan dog diet, beans provide a path to decreasing the risk of many diseases.

Beet Root and Beet Greens: Both root and tops in beets are healthy. In fact, the top greens have even more important properties than the root, so don't throw them out if you happen to find a nice bunch at your farmers' market or supermarket. Tops can be lightly steamed and added to a meal. Beet root contains vitamins A, B, C, and B2. They also contain iron, calcium, potassium, and are considered one of the most valuable vegetables for detoxification. They are a natural anti-inflammatory. Beets also contain natural sugar, but don't leave them out of your dog's diet; instead, feed them small amounts in moderation. It's widely documented that beets have been historically used to treat a number of illnesses.

Bell Peppers: Whether green, red, yellow, orange, or the lesser-known chocolate brown, white, and purple, bell peppers contain a high amount of vitamins C and A. Red peppers have more vitamins and nutrients than the other color peppers because they contain lycopene. The level of carotene, like lycopene, is nine times higher in red peppers than the other colors. Red peppers also have twice the vitamin C content of green and yellow peppers. Both red and green peppers are high in para-coumaric acid, which is known to inhibit the development of stomach cancer. Red peppers contain vitamins A, C, and B6. They are also rich in antioxidants and fiber.

Berries: Berries may be little, but they are mighty giants loaded with antioxidants that pack a punch! Most fruits and vegetables contain some antioxidants, but berries are extremely high in antioxidants. They help fight oxidative stress caused by free radicals. Eating berries can improve a dog's skin and coat, and prevent many diseases. They are anti-inflammatory and aid in joint flexibility. Strawberries, blueberries, blackberries, and raspberries are powerful, dog-friendly superfoods. Because of their antioxidant properties, the National Foundation for Cancer Research suggests eating berries as they may reduce the risk of some types of cancer. A word of caution: Conventionally grown berries are sprayed with pesticides to control fungus.

Inorganic strawberries and blueberries can carry as many as 20 pesticide residues, which cannot be washed off. The bottom line is this: You should only feed your dog organic berries.

Brazil Nuts: Brazil nuts are actually considered a seed. They are a natural source of selenium, which helps promote normal functioning of the immune system and thyroid gland. Brazil nuts are one of the fattiest nuts, but contain important health benefits. One crushed nut on your dog's plant-based food per week is sufficient for a 10-pound dog, or see recipe for SuperSeedDust (page 144) to use as another option.

Broccoli: Broccoli contains vitamins A, D, C, B9, and K. Don't discard the stems, as they are loaded with nutrients. Peel stems with a potato peeler to remove the tougher outer layer, chop remaining stem finely, and cook lightly. Broccoli plays a vital role in healthy vision as well as with cellular and immune functioning. The American Institute for Cancer Research has listed broccoli along with other cruciferous vegetables as one of the foods that fight cancer.

Brussels Sprouts: Brussels sprouts contain excellent nutrients, including folate, manganese, choline, copper, potassium, phosphorus, and omega-3 fatty acids. They also contain vitamins A, K, B6, and B1. Brussels sprouts are at the top of the cruciferous list, making them a cancer-preventative component. A small, varied amount of cruciferous vegetables is recommended in your dog's diet.

Buckwheat: Buckwheat is a superfood packed with nutrition. It is considered a seed and is gluten-free. Buckwheat is low on the glycemic scale, and is rich in fiber, protein, manganese, magnesium, potassium, and B vitamins. Buckwheat is a good source of antioxidants and bioflavonoids.

Cabbage: Cabbage is known as a cruciferous vegetable and is said to be one of the healthiest foods on the planet. It's high in sulfur, which purifies the blood, and contains cholesterol-lowering benefits and minerals, including calcium, magnesium, potassium, and phosphorus, and vitamins A, C, E, K, and folate.

Carrots: Carrots are a great source of vitamins A, K, and fiber. Studies show that high carotenoids, beta-carotene, alpha-carotene, and lutein are effective in lowering the risk of heart disease. Carrots are good for eye health, oral hygiene, and bone strength.

Cauliflower: Cauliflower is a cruciferous vegetable full of antioxidants and may help to reduce inflammation, so dogs with arthritis might benefit. It is very high in vitamins C and K, as well as a source of protein, thiamin, riboflavin, niacin, magnesium, phosphorus, fiber, vitamin B6, folate, pantothenic acid, potassium, and manganese. It's low in calories and can be eaten raw or cooked.

Celery: Celery is known for lowering cholesterol. It also contains a high concentration of antioxidants known as flavonoids. It contains vitamins A, C, and K, as well as folate, choline, calcium, magnesium, potassium, and iron, and it may also freshen up your dog's breath.

Chard: Chard comes in a rainbow assortment of stem colors and is considered a superfood. It contains vitamins A and E, which contribute to skin health and a shiny coat. It is good for immune support and contains calcium, iron, potassium, and magnesium

Chia Seeds: Chia seeds are high in protein and contain healthy omega-3 fatty acids, fiber, antioxidants, copper, potassium, and calcium. The antioxidant properties in chia seeds are higher than blueberries. They also contain vitamins A, B, D, and E as well as minerals such as sulfur, iron, iodine, magnesium, manganese, niacin, and thiamine. Make sure that the chia seeds are ground up or soaked in water before feeding to your pup.

Cilantro: Cilantro possesses a good amount of antioxidants, culinary fiber, and vitamins. It is a source of minerals, including calcium, iron, manganese, and potassium. Vitamins include A, C, K, and B6. Cilantro also contains riboflavin, niacin, folic acid, and beta-carotene.

Coconut Oil: Coconut oil is a powerful and nutritious food source. Unprocessed virgin organic coconut oil has many health benefits, both internally and externally. It is antibacterial, antifungal, antiparasitic, antiviral, and immune-building. It can prevent infection and aid in digestion. It alleviates flea allergies, itchy skin, and arthritis. Coconut oil can be applied directly to hot spots. It has high-alkaline properties, purifies the blood, and is good for bad breath. Coconut oil is a high heat oil and may be used for cooking.

Cranberries: Cranberries are known to help prevent and cure urinary tract infections. They are loaded with vitamin C, folate, fiber, and vitamin E. Fresh cranberries can be found around Thanksgiving, which is a good time to buy and freeze them. Cranberries can also be found in supermarket freezers. They are worth keeping on hand to add to your dog's meal. Do not feed dried cranberries to your dog, as they could contain added sugar.

Cucumbers: Cucumbers contain vitamin A and are needed for respiratory, urinary, and gastrointestinal tract health. Cucumbers have calcium, which plays an important role in strong teeth and bones. They are 95 percent water, which helps to flush toxins from your dog's body.

Dulce and Kelp Seaweed: The minerals and trace elements in sea vegetables provide 56 minerals required for your dog's body, which is higher than spinach, kidney beans, peas, and apricots. Sea vegetables contain more calcium than kale or bok choy. Magnesium is higher in kelp than in collard greens, walnuts, bananas, and oatmeal. A dog's body understands how to absorb and utilize these essential nutrients. Sea vegetables are good for heart heath and skeletal health. They contain calcium, magnesium, potassium, iron, chromium, iodine, and copper.

When your dog eats sea veggies, their cells recognize this natural, harmonious, health-giving balance.

Fennel Seeds: Fennel seeds have a slight licorice flavor and can be calming to the digestive tract. Sprinkle ground fennel seeds on your dog's meal or add them to any recipe to help relieve gas or upset stomach. They can also help to fight parasites.

Flaxseed Meal: Flaxseed meal is made from ground flaxseeds. Whether seeds are golden or brown, they are a great source of vitamins, fiber, and minerals, and are an excellent source of fatty acids. Flaxseed meal contains linolenic acid and alpha-linolenic acid. They also contain minerals and vitamins including B1 (thiamine), B2 (riboflavin), B3 (niacin), B5 (pantothenic acid), B6, B9 (folate), C, calcium, iron, magnesium, potassium, and zinc. Flaxseed meal is a good dietary fiber. It has been called one of the healthiest foods on the planet, as it is known to reduce heart disease, stroke, and diabetes. These claims have been made due to their high omega-3 fatty acids, which are key forces against inflammation. Inflammation is the cause of many diseases, including heart disease, diabetes, and arthritis. Flaxseed meal contains both soluble and insoluble fiber, which has cholesterol-lowering effects. Always grind flaxseeds to a powder before mixing in with your dog's food. Dogs should not be fed the whole seed, as they could get stuck in their teeth, but more important, whole flaxseed cannot be digested to receive all the nutrients, so use only flaxseed meal or flaxseed oil.

Flaxseed Oil: Flaxseed oil is a good source of omega-3 fatty acids, which are essential fatty acids that are good for the skin and coat. Flaxseed oil is a more concentrated form of omega-3 fatty acids, but without the fiber. Make sure that you store the oil in an airtight dark container in the fridge.

Ginger: Ginger is known for alleviating symptoms of gastrointestinal disorders. It contains antioxidants and is an anti-inflammatory. It is effective in preventing motion sickness of any kind, including if your dog gets carsick. Just give them ginger 30 minutes before getting into the car. It also helps nausea if your dog is going through cancer treatments. Ginger aids in gas relief, arthritic pain, inflammation reduction, and heartworm prevention. To give your dog ginger in its raw form mixed into their food, scrape the skin off with a knife and microplane or mince very finely. Use ⅛ teaspoon for small dogs, and up to ¼ teaspoon for large dogs.

Green Beans: Green beans are a good source of plant fiber, vitamins K and C, and manganese. If your dog has a tendency to put on weight, then replacing some of their regular food with green beans is a great low-calorie way to fill them up and help them maintain a healthy weight. Many dogs enjoy frozen green beans.

Hemp Seeds or Hearts: Hemp is one of the most nutritionally complete food sources in the world. These small seeds contain essential amino acids and essential fatty acids. With its perfect ratio of omega-6 and omega-3, hemp seeds are a complete protein, rivaled only by spirulina. Hemp seeds are a great source of protein for vegan dogs. These tiny seeds are easily digested and contain 10 essential amino acids. This super seed contains zinc, phosphorus, and gamma-Linolenic acid, which is an anti-inflammatory. They support a healthy metabolism, as well as a good coat and fur. Their antioxidants, vitamin E complex, and trace minerals make hemp seeds an important component in anti-aging efforts.

Kale: Kale is an anti-inflammatory and is good for vision and eye health. Kale contains vitamins A, C, and K, and is rich in minerals, including calcium, iron, copper, magnesium, and potassium. It also contains small amounts of omega-3 fatty acids. It is in the cruciferous family along with cabbage, broccoli, cauliflower, and Brussels sprouts. Let your dog enjoy cruciferous vegetables, but use in rotation with other vegetables. If your dog has thyroid issues, kale should be lightly steamed.

Kimchi: Kimchi is a staple in Korean cuisine. It is traditionally a side dish of fermented vegetables. Our Kimchi for Dogs recipe (page 118) is made with cabbage and seasoned without salt. It is loaded with vitamins and "healthy bacteria" called lactobacilli.

Lentils: Lentils are a good source of high protein, magnesium, potassium, copper, fiber, and iron. They are especially good for dogs with diabetes, as the fiber can help stabilize blood sugar levels. The magnesium and folate in lentils can help lower the risk of heart disease. Combined with a grain, lentils make a complete protein and can provide a complete source of amino acids.

Melons (including cantaloupe, honeydew, and watermelon): Melons are potassium-rich and reduce the risk of kidney stones and bone loss. They are also abundant in vitamin C, a disease-fighting antioxidant. They are very hydrating and contain beta-carotene, which is capable of preventing heart disease. Feed melons to dogs as a snack and in moderation.

 Cantaloupe is very sweet and hydrating, and is full of nutrition, including fiber, beta-carotene, potassium, vitamins C, B complex, A, and folic acid. It is good for the heart and eyes.

 Honeydew has a high-water content and is, therefore, very hydrating. Honeydew contains vitamins B, C, and E, copper, and potassium. Like all fruits, feed it to your dog in moderation.

Watermelon has a name that says it all. With its high water content, this fruit, like the honeydew, is very hydrating. Watermelon contains lycopene, which is good for heart and bone health. It also contains vitamins A and C, potassium, beta-carotene, amino acid, and magnesium, plus it is low in calories. Flavonoids and carotenoids make this fruit a good choice for antioxidants and anti-inflammatory support.

Millet: Millet has a very high B-vitamin content. It contains iron, potassium, calcium, zinc, and magnesium. Millet has healthy sources of essential fats and helps with heart health. It protects against diabetes, and improves muscles. Millet is good for the digestive system and optimizes the immune system.

Mushrooms: Mushrooms come in 100,000 varieties, but not all of them are edible. Never feed your dog wild mushrooms; the mushrooms you find in your local market are considered non-toxic to dogs and humans. Button mushrooms are the most cultivated edible kind. They contain B12, copper, phosphorus, potassium, and selenium. Shiitake mushrooms are also safe to feed your dog. They are a rich source of protein as well as copper, folate, iron, magnesium, manganese, niacin, pantothenic acid, potassium, riboflavin, selenium, thiamin, zinc, and dietary fiber. They also contain enzymes including pepsin, which aids digestion. Reishi is another safe mushroom for your dog and is used for its many medicinal properties.

Nutritional Yeast: Nutritional yeast is a rich source of amino acids and minerals. Adding it to your dog's food can help repel fleas. There are high levels of vitamin B found in nutritional yeast. Look for one that has been fortified with vitamin B12. Nutritional yeast is not the same as brewer's yeast. See SuperYeastDust recipe on page 145.

Oatmeal: Oatmeal is a good source of soluble fiber. This can be beneficial for some older dogs that may have trouble maintaining bowel regularity. Oatmeal should be purchased gluten-free, as it is an alternative source of grain for dogs allergic to wheat. Keep in mind that oatmeal should always be fed cooked plain with no sugar or flavoring. Oatmeal contains protein, fiber, vitamins B5 and B9, and iron. Oatmeal lowers cholesterol, which could prevent heart disease.

Olive Oil: In moderation, olive oil can make a healthful addition to your dog's diet. Remember to rotate the oils you use, including flax and hemp oil, which should not be cooked or heated. Olive oil is rich in monounsaturated fats and can prevent or lessen the effects of cardiovascular disease and diabetes. Olive oil is good for your dog's immune system. It prevents free radicals and helps keep skin and coat healthy. It is especially good for senior dogs, as it helps circulation and brain function. Nutritionally, olive oil is best used as a dressing or finishing oil, but can be used for light cooking.

Parsley: Parsley is often added to dog treats as a breath freshener. We also suggest using small amounts sprinkled in food. Avoid using spring parsley, also known as wild carrot, which is toxic to dogs. Pregnant dogs should not consume parsley, as it can cause contractions to start. Always use culinary herbs when cooking.

Peanut Butter or Sunflower Butter: These nut butters are good for dogs, but not in excess and not all brands. While dogs love peanut butter, it should be used sparingly. When purchasing peanut butter for your dog, it is extremely important that you read the ingredient label to be sure there is no sugar or xylitol, which are both dangerous for dogs. Buy organic, salt-free peanut butter or, even better, make your own.

Pears: With its many varieties, pears are one of the highest sources of dietary fiber and vitamins C, K, B2, B3, and B6. Pears contain magnesium, potassium, calcium, and copper. They have anti-inflammatory properties that help protect our dogs from heart disease. This easily digested fruit is hypoallergenic and low in acid. Pears contain boron, which dogs need in order to retain calcium. Always feed fresh pears—not frozen—and remove seeds and stem before feeding to your dog.

Peas: Peas are a good source of vitamins A, B, and K. They contain potassium, phosphorus, magnesium, protein, and thiamin. Peas are a phytonutrient powerhouse high in antioxidants.

Pumpkin: Pumpkin is a good source of fiber and beta-carotene, which is a source of vitamin A. Pumpkin also contains vitamin C, zinc, and iron. Dogs need fiber in their diets and pumpkin helps with digestive regularity. Pumpkin improves muscle strength, moisturizes skin and coat, and helps to control parasites. Fresh pumpkin is best, but it can be purchased in a carton. Be sure there are no additives, salt, or pumpkin pie spices.

Pumpkin Seeds: Pumpkin seeds are good for your dog's overall health. They contain protein, fiber, amino acids, copper, iron, magnesium, phosphorus, calcium, potassium, niacin, and zinc. Raw, organic pumpkin seeds are used to treat parasites and intestinal worms. You can feed them as a treat whole, but for best digestion, grind them or make our SuperSeedDust on page 144.

Quinoa: Quinoa is a good source of protein and amino acids. When legumes such as beans or lentils are combined, they become a perfect protein. Quinoa contains alpha-linolenic acid and omega-3 fatty acids. It also contains vitamins and minerals including B, E, niacin, thiamin, and folate. It is anti-inflammatory and contains antioxidant properties. For best digestion, soak quinoa 4 hours or overnight before cooking.

Rice, Brown: Brown rice is much better to feed your dog than white rice, which is stripped of nutrients and added back in with "enriched" synthetic vitamins. Brown rice is rich in proteins, thiamine, magnesium, calcium, potassium, and fiber. It is low glycemic and reduces insulin spikes, making it good for dogs with diabetes. Brown rice contains iron, zinc, and magnesium.

Rice, Wild: Wild rice is a good source of protein and rich in minerals and fiber. It helps keep your dog's digestion smooth and lowers cholesterol. It contains essential minerals including phosphorus, zinc, and folate. Wild rice is good for bones and contains vitamins A, C, and B, which are essential for immunity building. Wild rice is gluten-free, and contains more protein than brown rice. Wild rice is actually a water grass seed and is ideal for diabetic dogs. It is rich in antioxidants, which can slow down aging. These small black seeds contain essential minerals including phosphorus, zinc, and folate, which are good for bone health.

Romaine lettuce: Romaine lettuce is one of the top picks for dark leafy greens. Not only does this leaf taste good, but it is packed full of essential vitamins including

A, K, C, B1, B2, and B6, as well as omega-3s, folate, fiber, manganese, potassium, iron, magnesium, calcium phosphate, and copper. The vitamin C, beta-carotene, folic acid, potassium, and fiber make romaine lettuce heart healthy.

Rosemary: Rosemary is often used in Mediterranean cooking and has many medicinal purposes. It's an anti-inflammatory, anti-fungal, and has antiseptic properties. It has the ability to improve memory, increase circulation, and protect the immune system. Among many other things, it can also repel insects. Avoid using rosemary and rosemary oil if your dogs have had any type of seizure or are pregnant.

Seaweed or Sea Vegetables (see also Dulce and Kelp above): Seaweed and sea vegetables are high in omega-3 fatty acids, which may prevent heart attacks and strokes. Seaweed is an ancient superfood. It contains minerals such as calcium, potassium, iodine, magnesium, and zinc. Seaweed is high in protein and contains vitamins A, C, B, fiber, and alpha-linolenic acid. It contains antiviral, antibacterial, and anti-inflammatory properties. It also aids in the prevention of degenerative diseases including cardiovascular and diabetes. Other seaweeds are arame, dulse, hijiki, kelp, kombu, and wakame. Powdered kelp and dulse can be purchased for adding to your dog's meal. Look for certified organic sea vegetables.

Spinach: Spinach is high in fiber, is energy-producing, and can boost brainpower. Although Popeye ate his spinach from a can, it's not suggested your dog do the same. Fresh is best. Spinach is loaded with phytonutrients, including carotenoids, which provide antioxidants and a host of vitamins and nutrients including vitamins K, C, A, and E, and iron, calcium, potassium, and phosphorus. Rotating your dog's greens is advised. Spinach contains oxalates, so use it moderately—but don't cut out these foods completely, as they contain many healthful nutrients. It can be eaten both raw and lightly steamed.

Spirulina: Spirulina is a member of the blue-green algae family and is a highly bioavailable, complete rich protein. It is one of the most nutritious and concentrated food sources on the planet. Spirulina contains vitamins B, B12, and K. It also contains calcium, iron, manganese, magnesium, potassium, selenium, and zinc. Buy the best quality possible; see information under *Supplementation* (page 43).

Sprouts: Sunflower and pea sprouts are packed full of nutrients, including protein, zinc, vitamins A, B, C, D, E, and K. They also contain minerals such as calcium, copper, iron, magnesium, potassium, phosphorus, and selenium. They are rich in antioxidants and have an alkalizing effect on the body.

Squash: Squash comes in many varieties, including pumpkin (see entry above), acorn, spaghetti, butternut, and zucchini. Squash is rich in manganese, potassium, and calcium. The antioxidants and anti-inflammatory benefits help reduce heart and kidney diseases. Squash contains vitamins A, B12, B6, C, calcium, iron, and magnesium. Zucchini squash, whether green or yellow, can be peeled, cooked, and added to a main meal bowl, or microplaned as a topping to a meal. Spaghetti, pumpkin, butternut, and acorn squash may be roasted or steamed and are all good for dogs on a grain-free diet.

Sunflower lecithin: This is preferred over soy lecithin. Sunflower lecithin is good for heart health. It can provide your dog with one of the most powerful antioxidants in the form of phosphatidylcholine. If your dog has arthritis, supplementing their diet with sunflower lecithin can have a positive impact, as it helps lubricate your dog's joints. It contains vitamins A, B1, choline, omega-3 and -6 fatty acids.

Sunflower seeds: Sunflower seeds may seem small, but they are packed with vitamins B1, B3, B6, E, folate, copper, magnesium, manganese, selenium, and phosphorus. These tiny seeds enhance the immune system and are anti-inflammatory, heart-healthy, and support strong bones and muscles. One ounce of sunflower seeds contains 5 grams of protein. Purchase raw—not salted or roasted sunflower seeds.

Sweet potatoes: Sweet potatoes are a source of dietary fiber. They contain beta-carotene, manganese, copper, pantothenic acid, potassium, biotin, and phosphorus. They also contain vitamins A, B6, B3, B1, B2, and C. Sweet potatoes are gentle on a dog's digestive system and are gluten-free and anti-inflammatory. Dogs love sweet potatoes!

Tahini: Tahini is made from ground sesame seeds. Tahini provides a source of protein, copper, manganese, iron, zinc, vitamin B1, and calcium. Tahini is good for heart health and is considered a healthy fat that is high in essential amino acids, which is the building block of protein.

Thyme: Thyme is not just flavorful, but is used therapeutically as well. Thyme may increase blood flow to the skin, as it contains thymol. Thyme increases blood flow, speeds healing, and helps inhibit the growth of fungus and bacteria. It relaxes respiratory muscles and is good for heart health. Thyme is a natural bug repellent, and is good for kennel cough and oral health.

Turmeric: Turmeric dates back thousands of years to China and India. It was used for curing ailments, along with other potent herbs. Herbs and spices can add a great deal of health benefits to our dog's diet. Turmeric is on the top of the list with its high-antioxidant protection against free radicals. Turmeric contains a compound called curcumin, which is its main active ingredient, along with vitamins A, C, and E, which have been shown to prevent cataracts. Turmeric is good for your dog's immune system, eyes, bones, joints, liver, digestive system, cholesterol, circulation, and heart health. Because of its antioxidant properties, turmeric can slow down the aging process. Turmeric is considered anti-inflammatory and can help fight diseases such as arthritis, diabetes, and more.

Wheat germ: Wheat germ is a source of fiber, vitamins B and E, potassium, iron, zinc, phosphorus, and selenium. It can boost your dog's heart health and stimulate antioxidants, which help increase your dog's immune system

Zucchini: See *Squash*.

Resources

———o———

SUPPLEMENTS AND SUPPLIES

Animals Essentials Seaweed Calcium (animalessentials.com or amazon.com)

Augustine Approved (augustineapproved.com.au): supplements and dog blog

Compassion Circle (compassioncircle.com): for Vegepet supplements

Curry 'N' Pepper (currynpepper.com): Ayurveda food and supplies for dogs

PawNosh (pawnosh.co): safe and sustainable pet bowls

Vegan Essentials (veganessentials.com): vegan supplies for humans and dogs

READ AND WATCH

Dogs Naturally (dogsnaturallymagazine.com)

Dr. Donna Kelleher, plant a garden for your dog, from Animal Planet: *Animal Cribs*
(youtube.com/watch?v=MUzVJahXbVw&feature=youtu.be)

VEGAN DOG RESOURCES

Andrew Knight (vegepets.info/index.html)

Dr. Armaiti May (veganvet.net)

Vegan Action (vegan.org)

Index

———o———

About the Authors

———o———

Mimi Kirk is a well-known raw-food plant-based chef, international speaker, coach, and consultant. She is the best-selling author of *Live Raw, Live Raw Around the World, The Ultimate Book of Modern Juicing,* and *Raw-Vitalize*. Her books have been printed in four languages. Mimi has appeared on national television shows including *Dr. Oz, The Doctors, The Steve Harvey Show,* and *The Rachael Ray Show*. For decades, she's advocated a plant-based diet for human health—and now she's advocating for dog health as well.

Lisa Kirk is a Certified Canine Herbalist and has a passion for gardening. She has loved dogs even before she could walk and received her first pup before she was a year old as a Christmas gift. One of her favorite hobbies as a kid was bringing home stray dogs and cats. Lisa enjoys volunteering with rescue organizations, fostering dogs, and advocating for their overall health and wellbeing. Co-writing *The Plant-Based Dog Food Revolution* with her mother reflects Lisa's unyielding desire to help dog lovers learn more about feeding fresh, plant-based food to their dogs so they can live a long healthy life.